P9-DNV-820

AN AMERICAN PLAGUE

THE FEDERAL GAZETTE.

City of Philadelphia.

AT a Meeting of the Corporation, August 28, 1793, called expressly to take into consideration the present alarming state of the city, the Mayor laid before the Board, the following letters and orders, which he had from time to time, issued upon the occasion; and which, at the request of the Corporation, are now laid before the public.

GENTLEMEN,

AS there is great reason to apprehend that a dangerous, infectious disorder now prevails in this city, it is the duty of every department of authority to take the most effectual precautions to prevent its spreading: And as the keeping the streets at this time as clean as possible may conduce to that desirable object, I require that you will immediately upon the receipt of this letter, employ the scavengers in making the streets and gutters in every part of the town as clean as possible, and that as fast as the filth be laid together, that it be *immediately hauled away*.

I recommend that they begin to clean first in Water street, and all the alleys and passages from thence into Front-street, and then proceed to clean the other more airy streets.

I expect that the inhabitants will have the satisfaction of seeing this business going on, this afternoon or to-morrow morning; any delay on your part will reasonably be considered as an improper attention to a very essential duty.

MATTHEW CLARKSON, *Mayor.*

Phila. Aug. 22, 1793.

City Commissioners.

GENTLEMEN,

WHILST the present contagious fever shall continue in this city, it will be proper that every precaution be taken, that can in any degree prevent its spreading; and as it may conduce to that desirable end, I desire that you will be particularly attentive, to cause all the streets, lanes and alleys, in every part of the City, to be kept in a constant state of cleanliness, and to cause the filth and dirt to be hauled away, as speedily as it is heaped together. In executing this duty, you must not confine yourselves to the times prescribed by the ordinance, but cause it to be done as much oftener as may be necessary, to keep them effectually clean. The extra expence attending this business, will be allowed in account.

MATTHEW CLARKSON, *Mayor.*

Philad. Aug. 27, 1793.

FOR THE FEDERAL GAZETTE.

MR. BROWN,

I WISH through the channel of your paper, for the good of the public, to introduce a hint to the Grave-Diggers of this city, to lay every corpse a proper depth under ground; as infectious disorders, are liable to be spread, when they are not above two feet under the earth, which I have reason to believe, has been some times the case.

MONITOR.

Aug. 30.

European Intelligence,

Received by the Ship Adriana, Captain Robertson.

[CONTINUED.]

LONDON, June 24.

Admiralty-Office, June 22, 1793.

Copy of a letter from Captain Edward Pellew, of his Majesty's ship La Nymphe, to Mr. Stephens, dated off Portland, June 19, 1793.

I have the honor to inform you, that, at day-light yesterday morning, I was so fortunate as to fall in with the National French Frigate, La Cleopatra, mounting forty guns, and manned with 320 men, commanded by Monsieur Jean Mullon, three days from St. Maloes, and had taken nothing.

We brought her to close action at half past six, and in fifty-five minutes took possession of her; the two ships having fallen on board each other, we boarded her from the quarter-deck, and struck her colours; and finding it impossible to clear the ships, then hanging head and stern, we came to anchor, which divided us, after we had received on board 150 prisoners. The enemy fought us like brave men, neither ship firing a shot until we had hailed.—Her captain was killed, three lieutenants wounded; the number of men not yet ascertained, but, from the best accounts, about sixty; her mizen-mast overboard, and her tiller shot off.

I am extremely concerned she was not purchased at a less expence of valuable officers and men on our part, whose gallantry I cannot sufficiently regret, and to whose loss I cannot possibly do justice. We had twenty-three men killed, and twenty-seven men wounded, of which a list is enclosed.

I am very particularly indebted to my first lieutenant, Mr. Amherst Morris, and no less so to leiutenants George Luke and Richard Pellew, and I was ably seconded on the quarter-deck by

but it is not for these that I claim generosity of the English Nation.

"Your Lordship will see that it necessity alone that made me chang name, when I came to seek an asy in England. I respect the Laws. fiction I made use of when at D was merely local, and I hasten pair it by a true declaration of my

"If my request can be grant will comply with whatever the prud of the Minister shall require of me,

"I have the honour to be, &c.

(Signed) "DUMOURIE

Lord GRENVILLE's ANSWE

"*Whitehall, June* 16, 179

"I received, Sir, this morning, Letter you did me the honour dress to me. It is the business Secretary of State for the Home partment to take the orders of His jesty relative to the residence of A in this Kingdom, and to notify the officially; but as it is to me that have addressed yourself on this occa I cannot do otherwise than ack ledge the receipt of your Letter answer the demands which it con

"Your stay in England will be ject to too many inconvenienc make it possible for the Governme this Country to permit it. I canno regret, that you had not gained i mation in this particular before came to England. If your wi been made known to me befo undertook the journey, I would informed you without reserve, th would have been a useless one. mains now with me to point out my opinion, that you must co without delay, to the decision I been under the necessity to com cate to you by this Letter.

"I have the honour to be, &c

(Signed) "GRENVILL

M. DUMOURIER.

About the middle of the da Thursday last, a dreadful fire brok at Stanton St John's, about four from Oxford, which entirely dest twenty-one dwelling-houses, five and divers other out buildings, by many of the inhabitants are redu the utmost distress.

Commercial Failures.

THE malicious and absurd at to charge the late commercial fa to the account of the war is pr exposed in the following observ introduced into the fourth editi Mr. Bowles's Real Grounds of the

"Imported however as the wa its object, and just in its principl most illiberal endeavours are m enhance its difficulties, to depr its advantages, to darken its pro

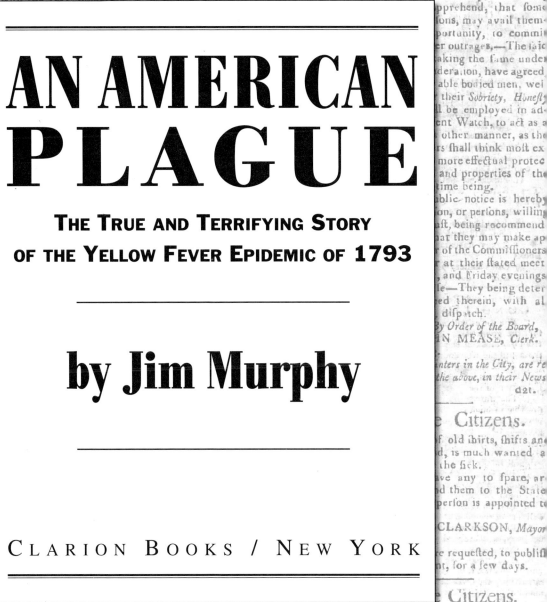

AN AMERICAN PLAGUE

The True and Terrifying Story of the Yellow Fever Epidemic of 1793

by Jim Murphy

Clarion Books / New York

Clarion Books
a Houghton Mifflin Company imprint
215 Park Avenue South, New York, NY 10003

The text was set in 12-point Times Roman.
Book design by Trish Parcell Watts.
Map by Kayley LeFaiver.

www.houghtonmifflinbooks.com

Printed in the U.S.A.

Library of Congress Cataloging-in-Publication Data
Murphy, Jim
An American plague : the true and terrifying story of the yellow fever epidemic of 1793 / by Jim Murphy.
p. cm.
ISBN 0-395-77608-2 (alk. paper)
1. Yellow fever—Pennsylvania—Philadelphia—History—18th century—Juvenile literature. [1. Yellow fever—Pennsylvania—Philadelphia—History—18th century. 2. Pennsylvania—History—1775–1865.] I. Title.
RA644.Y4 M875 2003
614.5'41'097481109033—dc21 2002151355

VB 10 9 8 7 6 5 4 3

For Mike and Ben—my wonderful, at-home germ machines. This one's for you!

With love, Dad

CONTENTS

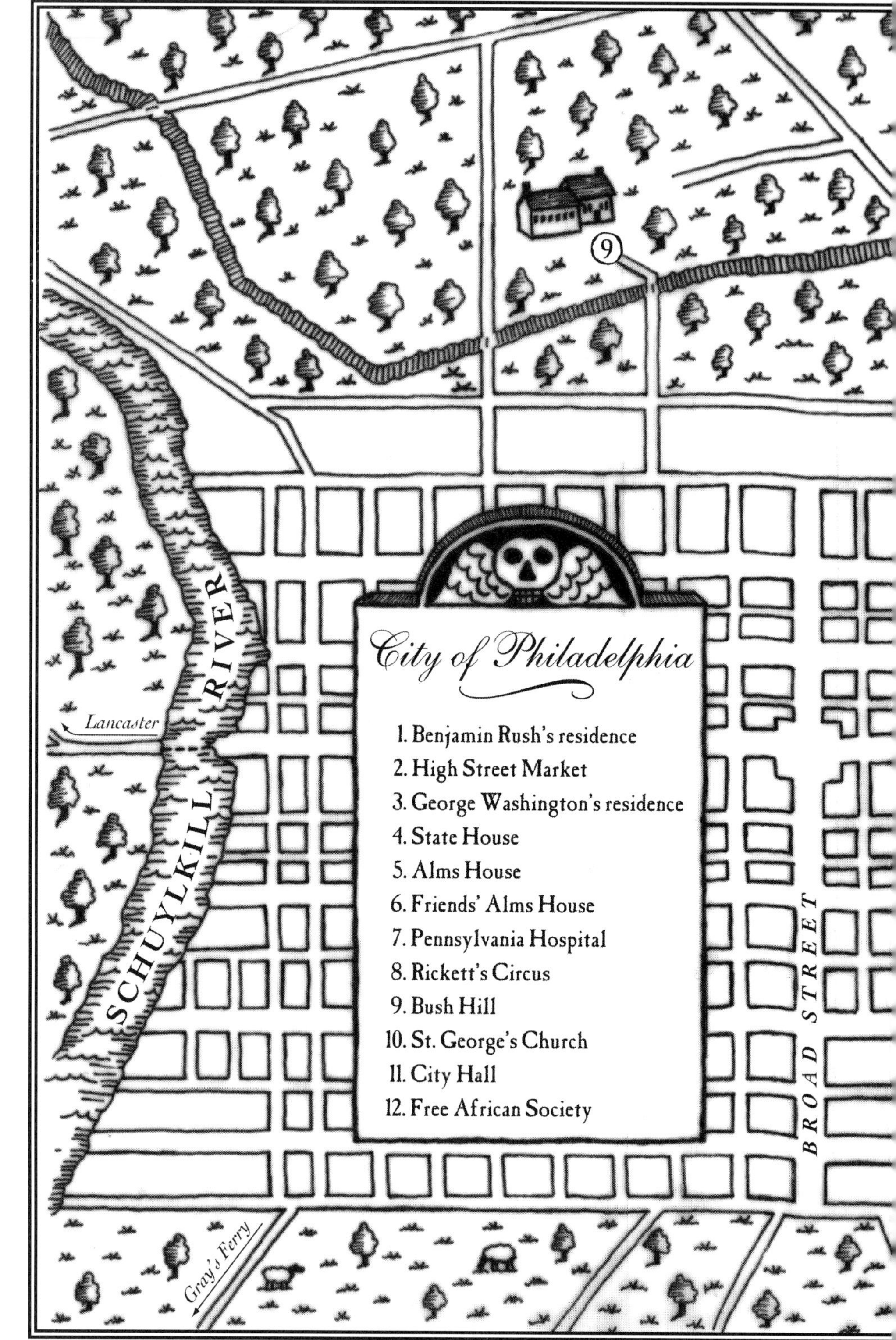
City of Philadelphia
1. Benjamin Rush's residence
2. High Street Market
3. George Washington's residence
4. State House
5. Alms House
6. Friends' Alms House
7. Pennsylvania Hospital
8. Rickett's Circus
9. Bush Hill
10. St. George's Church
11. City Hall
12. Free African Society
9
SCHUYLKILL RIVER
Lancaster
Gray's Ferry
BROAD STREET

Northern Liberties
Township
Germantown
RACE STREET
ARCH STREET
HIGH (MARKET) STREET
WATER
STREET
WALNUT STREET
SPRUCE STREET
LOMBARD STREET
5TH STREET
DELAWARE RIVER
Southwark Township
1
2
3
4
5
6
7
8
10
11
12

Warner Swen, laſt and heel maker, 24, Cheſnut St.
Warner Joſeph, laſt and heel maker, 14, Cheſnut St.
Warner Ann, 20, Mulberry St.
Warner John, ivory turner and whale-bone cutter, 28, No. Fourth St.
Warner James, hair-ſieve maker, 1, Coombes's alley
Warner Heronimus, braſs founder, 26, No. Eigth St.
Warren James, ſhip carpenter, 420, So. Front St.
Warren Mary, ſchoolmiſtreſs, Shepherd's alley
Warrington Benjamin, labourer, 19, Plumb St. Southwark
Warrington Cæſar, labourer, 123, Pine St.
Wart Eſther, widow, Saſſafras near Broad St.
Warts Jacob, labourer, 16, Plumb St. Southwark
Wartman Adam, merchant, 169, No. Third St.
WASHINGTON GEORGE, *Preſident of the United States*, 190, High St.
Waſſem Chriſtopher, labourer, 23, Vernon St.
Waterman Jeſſe, ſchoolmaſter, 103, Cheſnut St.
Waters Thomas, gentleman, 69, No. Second St.
Waters Nathaniel, hatter, 87, No. Second St.
Waters John, ſchoolmaſter, 272, So. Second St.
Waters Thomas, well digger back, 154, Spruce St.
Watkins James, joiner, 121, Mulberry St.
Watkins Thomas, bruſhmaker, 13, Strawberry St.
Watkins John, boot and ſhoemaker, 17, Cedar St.
Watkins David, grocer, Crab lane, near Shippen St. Southwark
Watkins William, tobacconiſt, 167, So. Front, and 166, So. Water St.
Watſon John, clerk in the bank of North America, 254, High St.
Watſon Charles C. taylor, 93, So. Second St.
Watſon Margaret, milliner, 177, So. Second St.
Watſon William, ſea captain, 58, Duke St. No. Lib.
Watſon Thomas, grocer, 48, Lombard St.
Watſon Benjamin, copperſmith, 140, So. Fourth St.
Watts George, ſea captain, 13, Vernon St.
Way George ſen. coachmaker, 79, Dock St.
Way Andrew, taylor, 1, Quarry St.
Way George jun. coachmaker, 25, Carter's alley
Wayne Elizabeth, widow, 440, So. Front St.
Wayne Samuel, houſe carpenter, 13, Key's alley
Wayne William, lumber merchant, 166, No. Front St.
Wayne Jacob, cabinet and chair maker, 162, No. Front and 17, Key's alley
Weatherby Samuel, corder of wood, 82, No. Water St.
Weatherby Margaret, widow, 3, Strawberry St.
Weatherſtone Peter, hoſtler, 393, No. Second St.
Weatherſtone John, butcher, corner of Crown and Vine Sts.

CHAPTER ONE

No One Noticed

About this time, this destroying scourge, the malignant fever, crept in among us.

—MATHEW CAREY, NOVEMBER 1793

Saturday, August 3, 1793. The sun came up, as it had every day since the end of May, bright, hot, and unrelenting. The swamps and marshes south of Philadelphia had already lost a great deal of water to the intense heat, while the Delaware and Schuylkill Rivers had receded to reveal long stretches of their muddy, root-choked banks. Dead fish and gooey vegetable matter were exposed and rotted, while swarms of insects droned in the heavy, humid air.

In Philadelphia itself an increasing number of cats were dropping dead every day, attracting, one Philadelphian complained, "an amazing number of flies and other insects." Mosquitoes were everywhere, though their high-pitched whirring was particularly loud near rain barrels, gutters, and open sewers.

These sewers, called "sinks," were particularly ripe this year. Most streets in the city were unpaved and had no system of covered sewers

OPPOSITE: *From James Hardie's* Philadelphia Directory and Register, *1793.* (THE LIBRARY COMPANY OF PHILADELPHIA)

and pipes to channel water away from buildings. Instead, deep holes were dug at various street corners to collect runoff water and anything else that might be washed along. Dead animals were routinely tossed into this soup, where everything decayed and sent up noxious bubbles to foul the air.

Down along the docks lining the Delaware, cargo was being loaded onto ships that would sail to New York, Boston, and other distant ports. The hard work of hoisting heavy casks into the hold was accompanied by the stevedores' usual grunts and muttered oaths.

The men laboring near Water Street had particular reason to curse. The sloop *Amelia* from Santo Domingo had anchored with a cargo of

The ferryboat (right) from Camden, New Jersey, has just arrived at the busy Arch Street dock. (THE HISTORICAL SOCIETY OF PENNSYLVANIA)

coffee, which had spoiled during the voyage. The bad coffee was dumped on Ball's Wharf, where it putrefied in the sun and sent out a powerful odor that could be smelled over a quarter mile away. Benjamin Rush, one of Philadelphia's most celebrated doctors and a signer of the Declaration of Independence, lived three long blocks from Ball's Wharf, but he recalled that the coffee stank "to the great annoyance of the whole neighborhood."

Despite the stench, the streets nearby were crowded with people that morning—ship owners and their captains talking seriously, shouting children darting between wagons or climbing on crates and barrels, well-dressed men and women out for a stroll, servants and slaves hurrying from one chore to the next. Philadelphia was then the largest city in North America, with nearly 51,000 inhabitants; those who didn't absolutely have to be indoors working had escaped to the open air to seek relief from the sweltering heat.

Many of them stopped at one of the city's 415 shops, whose doors and windows were wide open to let in light and any hint of a cooling breeze. The rest continued along, headed for the market on High Street.

Here three city blocks were crowded with vendors calling their wares while eager shoppers studied merchandise or haggled over weights and prices. Horse-drawn wagons clattered up and down the cobblestone street, bringing in more fresh vegetables, squawking chickens, and squealing pigs. People commented on the stench from Ball's Wharf, but the market's own ripe blend of odors—of roasting meats, strong cheeses, days-old sheep and cow guts, dried blood, and horse manure—tended to overwhelm all others.

One and a half blocks from the market was the handsomely refurbished mansion of Robert Morris, a wealthy manufacturer who had used his fortune to help finance the Revolutionary War. Morris was lending this house to George and Martha Washington and had moved himself into another, larger one he owned just up the block. Washington

Rich and poor do their food shopping along Market Street.
(THE LIBRARY COMPANY OF PHILADELPHIA)

was then president of the United States, and Philadelphia was the temporary capital of the young nation and the center of its federal government. Washington spent the day at home in a small, stuffy office seeing visitors, writing letters, and worrying. It was the French problem that was most on his mind these days.

Not so many years before, the French monarch, Louis XVI, had sent money, ships, and soldiers to aid the struggling Continental Army's fight against the British. The French aid had been a major reason why Washington was able to surround and force General Charles Cornwallis to surrender at Yorktown in 1781. This military victory eventually led to a British capitulation three years later and to freedom for the United States—and lasting fame for Washington.

Then, in 1789, France erupted in its own revolution. The common people and a few nobles and churchmen soon gained complete power in

France and beheaded Louis XVI in January 1793. Many of France's neighbors worried that similar revolutions might spread to their countries and wanted the new French republic crushed. Soon after the king was put to death, revolutionary France was at war with Great Britain, Holland, Spain, and Austria.

Naturally, the French republic had turned to the United States for help, only to have President Washington hesitate. Washington knew that he and his country owed the French an eternal debt. He simply wasn't sure that the United States had the military strength to take on so many formidable foes.

Many citizens felt Washington's Proclamation of Neutrality was a betrayal of the French people. His own secretary of state, Thomas Jefferson, certainly did, and he argued bitterly with Treasury Secretary Alexander Hamilton over the issue. Wasn't the French fight for individual freedom, Jefferson asked, exactly like America's struggle against British oppression?

The situation was made worse in April by the arrival of the French republic's new minister, Edmond Charles Genêt. Genêt's first action in the United States was to hire American privateers, privately owned and manned ships, to attack and plunder British ships in the name of his government. He then traveled to Philadelphia to ask George Washington to support his efforts. Washington gave Genêt what amounted to a diplomatic cold shoulder, meeting with him very briefly, but refusing to discuss the subject of United States support of the French. But a large number of United States citizens loved Genêt and the French cause and rallied around him.

Pro-French sympathies were further heightened in July by the sudden influx of 2,100 French refugees, who were fleeing a fierce slave rebellion in Santo Domingo. Pro-French demonstrations were held near the president's home and escalated in intensity. Vice President John

Adams was extremely nervous about this "French Madness" and recalled that "ten thousand people in the streets of Philadelphia . . . threatened to drag Washington out of his house, and effect a revolution in the government or compel it to declare war in favor of the French Revolution."

While Washington worried, the city's taverns, beer gardens, and coffeehouses—all 176 of them—were teeming with activity that Saturday. There men, and a few women, lifted their glasses in toasts and singing and let the hours slip away in lively conversation. Business and politics and the latest gossip were the favorite topics. No doubt the heat, the foul stink from Ball's Wharf, and the country's refusal to join with France were discussed and argued over at length.

In all respects it seemed as if August 3 was a very normal day, with business and buying and pleasure as usual.

Oh, there were a few who felt a tingle of unease. For weeks an unusually large supply of wild pigeons had been for sale at the market. Popular folklore suggested that such an abundance of pigeons always brought with it unhealthy air and sickness.

Dr. Rush had no time for such silly notions, but he, too, sensed that something odd was happening. His concern focused on a series of illnesses that had struck his patients throughout the year—the mumps in January, jaw and mouth infections in February, scarlet fever in March, followed by influenza in July. "There was something in the heat and drought," the good doctor speculated, "which was uncommon, in their influence upon the human body."

The Reverend J. Henry C. Helmuth of the Lutheran congregation, too, thought something was wrong in the city, though it had nothing to do with sickness of the body. It was the souls of its citizens he worried about. "Philadelphia . . . seemed to strive to exceed all other places in the breaking of the Sabbath," he noted. An increasing number of people shunned church and went instead to the taverns, where they drank and

A group of well-to-do men gather at the City Tavern to drink, smoke their pipes, and talk away the afternoon. (THE LIBRARY COMPANY OF PHILADELPHIA)

gambled; too many others spent their free time in theaters which displayed "rope-dancing and other shows." Sooner or later, he warned, the city would feel God's displeasure.

Rush and Helmuth would have been surprised to know that their worries were turning to reality on August 3. For on that Saturday a young French sailor rooming at Richard Denny's boarding house, over on North Water Street, was desperately ill with a fever. Eighteenth-century record keeping wasn't very precise, so no one bothered to write

One of the many narrow, forgotten alleys of Philadelphia.

(The Historical Society of Pennsylvania)

down his name. Besides, this sailor was poor and a foreigner, not the sort of person who would draw much attention from the community around him. All we know is that his fever worsened and was accompanied by violent seizures, and that a few days later he died.

Other residents at Denny's would follow this sailor to the grave—a Mr. Moore fell into a stupor and passed away, Mrs. Richard Parkinson expired on August 7, next the lodging house owner and his wife, Mary, and then the first sailor's roommate. Around the same time, two people in the house next to Denny's died of the same severe fever.

Eight deaths in the space of a week in two houses on the same street . . . but the city did not take notice. Summer fevers were common visitors to all American cities in the eighteenth century, and therefore not headline news. Besides, Denny's was located on a narrow out-of-the-way street—really more an alley than a street. "It is much confined," a resident remarked, "ill-aired, and, in every respect, is a disagreeable street." Things happened along this street all the time—sometimes very bad things—that went unnoticed by the authorities and the rest of the population.

So the deaths did not disrupt Philadelphia much at all. Ships came and went; men and women did chores, talked, and sought relief from the heat and insects; the markets and shops hummed with activity; children played; and the city, state, and federal governments went about their business.

No one noticed that the church bells were tolling more often than usual to announce one death, and then another. They rang for Dr. Hugh Hodge's little daughter, for Peter Aston, for John Weyman, for Mary Shewell, and for a boy named McNair. No one knew that a killer was already moving through their streets with them, an invisible stalker that would go house to house until it had touched everyone, rich or poor, in some terrible way.

it is guaranteed,
.
y, that from se-
nt, passed in the
I. and Edward
led, it appears,
asing arms, and
ed for the use of
m being illegal,
, that it was ex-
orced by penal-

y, that no assem-
illegal, unless it
t, or meets, with
one.
y, that to assem-
uthorized by the
al act.
ly, that to assist
agistrate, in the
mobs, is so far
to, that it is re-

y, that shewing
niversary of the
ved sovereign in
hibited by law,

y, that we regret
rrived, when any
e anniversary of
present majesty,
y his ministers, as
fection to the go-
use the people ex-
al privilege of be-
not prohibited,
enalties, even in
e IVth.
ly, that however
er constitutional
ns, we will not
is city by firing
of June next, but
stitution, we de-
ys ready armed
the civil magis-
on of the peace of
determined spirit
o support and de-
the constitution,
t we will never
t with our lives.

E D,
VANT MAN, who
care of Horses and
ire at the office of
dtf.

declaration ... have never intima-ted to you an intention of appealing to the people; that it is not true that a difference in political sentiments has ever betrayed me to forget what was due to your character or to the exalted reputation you had acquired by humbling a tyrant against whom you fought in the cause of liberty." A publication of your answer will be the only reply which shall be given to those party men, who never fail to confound the individual with affairs of state, which they too often make use of as a pretext for their zeal, and a reason for dastardly appearing under anonymous signatures.

As to myself, I have always openly declared what I thought, and signed what I had written, and if others have supposed they could advance my views, by newspaper publications and paragraphs, they are much deceived—A good cause needs no advance—Time and Truth will make it triumph, and ours must triumph in spite of its implacable enemies, and the present cold indifference of some who were its ancient friends.

I have the honor, &c.

Mr. JEFFERSON'S ANSWER.

Philadelphia, August 16, 1793.

SIR,

THE President of the United States, has received the letter which you addressed to him from New-York, on the 13th inst. and I am desired to observe to you, that it is not the established course for the diplomatic characters residing here, to have any direct correspondence with him—The Secretary of state, is the organ through which their communication should pass.

The President does not conceive it to be within the line of propriety or duty for him, to bear evidence *against* a declaration which, whether made to him or others is perhaps immaterial, he, therefore, declines interfering in the case.

I have the honor to be with great respect,
SIR,
Your most obedient,
And most humble servant,
THOMAS JEFFERSON.

The Minister Plenipotentiary of the Republic of France.

Excellency being ... was unfortunately prevented from attending. A salute from the Frigate and a return from the castle anounced their departure.

Previous to the departure of the company, a deputation of the officers and crew of the ship, waited on his honor the Lieutenant-governor, and after a very polite address, placed the cap of liberty on his venerable head, as a token of their respect and esteem for the republican virtues of that truly patriotic character,

The next day, the Selectmen paid a visit to the captain and officers on board, and were also welcomed by a salute.

On Friday last, the gentlemen Selectmen, accompanied (in compliance with an invitation) by citizens Duplaine, Van Dogen and a number of public & private gentlemen of this town, paid a visit to the Islands in the outer-harbour and partook of a republican entertainment on Rainsford's Island, previously prepared. They were honoured with a salute in passing the Castle.

THE FEDERAL GAZETTE.

On Tuesday last departed this life in the 33d year of her age, Mrs. CATHERINE LE MAIGRE, wife of Mr. Peter Le Maigre, of this city, merchant.

Exemplary in every social and domestic relation, endeared to all who knew her, as well by her engaging and unaffected manners, as by the sincerity and benevolence of her heart, few have descended to the tomb more sincerely and more deservedly regretted: But while wounded friendship heaves the sigh, while bleeding affection bedews with tears the grave of departed worth, Religion holds up the consoling reflection, "*that* the close of a life of virtue is the commencement of a life of endless felicity."—

AT this unhealthy season, it becomes the duty and interest of every citizen to contribute all in his power to prevent the spreading of disorders.

The Fire Companies would render essential service upon this occasion, if they would cause their engines to be exercised daily, until rain shall fall, in wetting the streets, which at the same time would prevent their getting out of order for want of use.

CHAPTER TWO

"All Was Not Right"

8 or 10 persons buried out of Water St. between Race and Arch Sts.; many sick in our neighborhood, and in ye City generally.

—Elizabeth Drinker, August 21, 1793

Monday, August 19. It was clear that thirty-three-year-old Catherine LeMaigre was dying, and dying horribly and painfully. Between agonized gasps and groans she muttered that her stomach felt as if it were burning up. Every ten minutes or so her moaning would stop abruptly and she would vomit a foul black bile.

Her husband, Peter, called in two neighborhood doctors to save his young wife. One was Dr. Hugh Hodge, whose own daughter had been carried off by the same fever just days before. Hodge had been an army surgeon during the Revolutionary War, and while stubborn and crusty in his ways, he was a respected physician. The other was Dr. John Foulke, who was a fellow of Philadelphia's prestigious College of Physicians and a member of the Pennsylvania Hospital board.

Hodge and Foulke did what they could for their patient. They gave her cool drinks of barley water and apple water to reduce the fever, and

Opposite: *From* The Federal Gazette, *August 23, 1793.*
(The Library Company of Philadelphia)

red wine with laudanum to help her rest. Her forehead, face, and arms were washed regularly with damp cloths.

Nothing worked, and Catherine LeMaigre's condition worsened. Her pulse slowed, her eyes grew bloodshot, her skin took on the pale-yellow color that gave the disease its name. More black vomit came spewing forth. In desperation, the two physicians sent for their esteemed colleague Dr. Benjamin Rush.

Rush was forty-seven years old and so highly respected that he was often called in by colleagues when they were baffled by a case. His medical training had been extensive, consisting of five years of apprenticeship with the pre-eminent doctor in the United States, John Redman. After this he had gone to Europe to study under the most skilled surgeons and doctors in the western world.

He was passionate and outspoken in his beliefs, no matter what the subject. He opposed slavery, felt that alcohol and tobacco should be avoided, urged that the corporal punishment of children be stopped, and thought that the best way to keep a democracy strong was by having universal education. Along with his beliefs went an unimaginable amount of energy. Despite a persistent cough and weak lungs that often left him gasping for air, he worked from early in the morning until late at night—writing letters and papers, visiting patients, reading the latest medical literature, or attending to any one of a number of institutions and charities he belonged to.

Hodge and Foulke told Rush about Catherine LeMaigre's symptoms and what they had done to help her. There was nothing much else they could do, Rush said, after the three men left her bedchamber to discuss the case. Rush then noted that in recent days he had seen "an unusual number of bilious fevers, accompanied with symptoms of uncommon malignity." In a grave voice, his seriousness reflected in his intense blue eyes, he added that "all was not right in our city."

The two other doctors agreed, and then all three recounted the symptoms they had seen. The sickness began with chills, headache, and a painful aching in the back, arms, and legs. A high fever developed, accompanied by constipation. This stage lasted around three days, and then the fever suddenly broke and the patient seemed to recover.

But only for a few short hours.

The next stage saw the fever shoot up again. The skin and eyeballs

---

This French watercolor, done in 1819, is perhaps the first illustration to show a yellow fever victim in the early stages of the illness. (THE COLLEGE OF PHYSICIANS OF PHILADELPHIA)

turned yellow, as red blood cells were destroyed, causing the bile pigment bilirubin to accumulate in the body; nose, gums, and intestines began bleeding; and the patient vomited stale, black blood. Finally, the pulse grew weak, the tongue turned a dry brown, and the victim became depressed, confused, and delirious.

Rush noted another sign as well: tiny reddish eruptions on the skin.

Clearly, things have gone from bad to worse for the fever patient.

(THE COLLEGE OF PHYSICIANS OF PHILADELPHIA)

"They appeared chiefly on the arms, but they sometimes extended to the breast." Physicians called these sores petechiae, which is Latin for skin spots, and Rush observed that they "resembled moscheto bites."

Hodge then pointed out that the deaths, including his daughter's, had all happened on or near Water Street. Foulke told of other deaths along the street and said he knew the origin of the fevers: the repulsive smell in the air caused by the rotting coffee on Ball's Wharf.

The idea that illness was caused by microscopic organisms, such as bacteria and viruses, was not known at the time. Instead, doctors based their medical thinking on the 2,500-year-old Greek humoral theory. This concept stated that good health resulted when body fluids, called humors, were in balance. The humors were phlegm, choler, bile, and blood.

Disease arose from an imbalance of these humors—too much of one, not enough of another. Any number of things could cause this condition, such as poor diet, excess drinking, poison, or a dog bite, to name just a few. Even bad news could unsettle the humors and cause illness. So it made sense to Rush, Hodge, and Foulke that the putrid-smelling air could upset people enough to cause an outbreak of violent, fatal fevers.

Rush, however, sensed something else. The symptoms he was seeing reminded him of a sickness that had swept through Philadelphia back in 1762, when he was sixteen years old and studying under Dr. Redman. Rush was never shy with his opinions, and standing there in the LeMaigres' parlor, he boldly announced that the disease they now confronted was the dreaded yellow fever.

Putting the name yellow fever to the illness was not to be done lightly. Yellow fever was one of the most vicious diseases in the world and could create panic anywhere. It appeared suddenly, savaged its victims' bodies, and—because there was absolutely no cure—killed at an alarming pace. While mortality rates for yellow fever varied widely, it was not unusual for it to kill 50 percent of those who contracted it. What is more, the stench of a yellow fever victim's bodily evacuations and breath, the odor from their soiled clothes and bed linens, and even the air that escaped from their sickroom was believed by many to spread the disease with lightning speed.

Rush had, in short, announced that Philadelphia was in the grip of a deadly, unstoppable plague.

Hodge and Foulke thought they and their colleagues needed to see and discuss many more fever cases before putting a name to the disease, especially such a terrifying name. A mistake would disrupt the workings of the city for no reason. Rush understood this well, but he did not waver from his diagnosis. Once his mind was made up, he rarely changed it.

After Rush left the LeMaigres' home, he made it a point to tell his friends about the reappearance of yellow fever, and he advised them all to leave the city. He visited the mayor of Philadelphia, Matthew Clarkson, and the governor of Pennsylvania, Thomas Mifflin, to inform them as well. Next he went about town to confer with other doctors.

On Monday, August 19, and for several days after this, the fever was still pretty much confined to the Water Street area near Ball's Wharf. Only a handful of doctors had encountered it firsthand. Therefore, most of the city's eighty physicians did not believe that the illness described by Rush was indeed yellow fever. They felt that the disorder must be one of the other common fevers that often struck during warm weather. Among the possibilities mentioned were jail fever, camp fever, eruptive military fever, and autumnal fever. Any one of these could cause violent physical suffering and death.

Rush was annoyed that his diagnosis and warnings were being "treated with ridicule or contempt," but he shrugged off these doctors as ignorant. They would come around to his view in time, he knew. He only hoped it wouldn't be too late.

Meanwhile, the deaths kept coming at an alarming rate. Catherine LeMaigre died on Tuesday, despite the efforts of her three highly skilled physicians. On Wednesday twelve more died; thirteen died on Thursday.

Others besides the doctors were beginning to notice the illness. The Reverend J. Henry C. Helmuth found himself visiting more and more of his congregation with fevers of a "most dangerous complexion." He stopped by the home of a man that Monday and made sure he was well taken care of and comfortable. "Nevertheless to my very great surprise, he was a corpse on the 20th," Helmuth reported bluntly.

"'Tis a sickly time now in Philada," another citizen, Elizabeth Drinker, wrote, "and there has been an unusual number of funerals lately here." A few days later she would add, "'Tis really an alarming and serious time."

"The fever has assumed a most alarming appearance," Rush wrote to his wife, Julia, who was summering in Princeton with their youngest children. "It not only mocks in most instances the power of medicine, but it has spread thro' several parts of the city remote from the spot where it originated."

Not just the fever spread; word of it spread as well. That Thursday, Mayor Clarkson placed a notice in the newspapers saying there was "great reason to apprehend that a dangerous infectious disorder" was loose in the city. He ordered laborers hired by the city, called scavengers, to clean the streets of decaying garbage and dead animals, since their vile smell might well be causing the disease.

Governor Mifflin was equally upset. The state legislature was scheduled to assemble on Tuesday, August 27, and he was to deliver a formal speech on the condition of Pennsylvania. Should the meeting be canceled, he wondered, if the fever really was so dangerous? And should he and his family leave the city? He then asked that the health officer of the port and the port physician investigate the disorder and issue a report.

Both the mayor and the governor wanted to confront and contain the disease as quickly as possible. They also wanted to keep the citizens of Philadelphia calm by showing that they were taking firm steps to deal with the problem. But it was already too late.

Thursday's newspapers had been read by thousands of individuals. These people spoke with neighbors and friends and business associates about the "dangerous, infectious disorder." This group then spread the alarming news even further. The city's taverns buzzed with talk of the strange, killing fever, as did the street markets and shops.

Rain fell on Saturday, but it didn't stop the death carts from rumbling through the streets carrying seventeen more people to their graves.

John Hills's 1796 map of Philadelphia shows how densely settled the streets and alleys near the Delaware River had become. (THE LIBRARY COMPANY OF PHILADELPHIA)

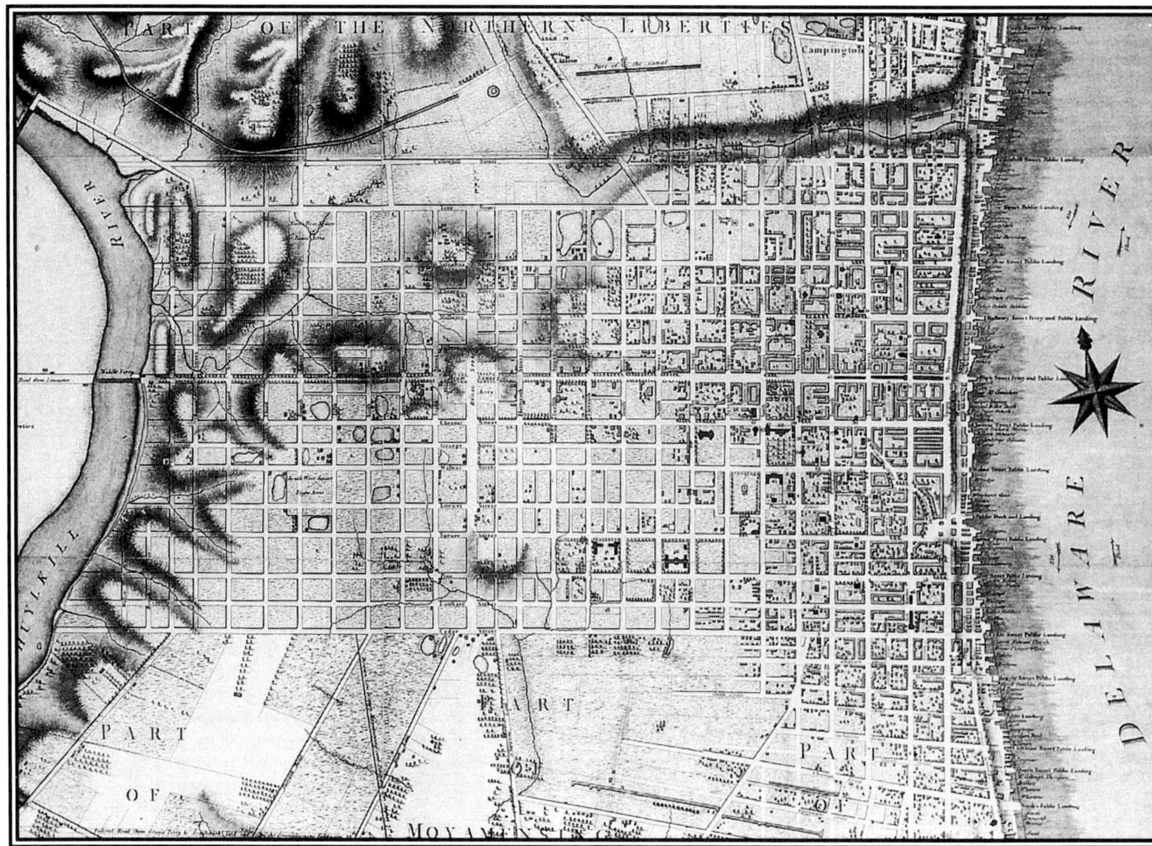

"They are a Dieing on our right hand & on our left," wrote twenty-one-year-old Isaac Heston to his brother, "we have it oposit us, in fact, all around us. Great are the number . . . Calld to the grave."

Fear, it seemed, was spreading even faster than the disease.

On Sunday, August 25, a savage storm hit the city, bringing winds and torrents of rain. Water cascaded off roofs, splashed loudly onto the sidewalks, and ran in burbling rivers through the streets. The howling wind and pounding rain made a frightful noise, and yet through it all a single, chilling sound could still be heard—the awful tolling of the church bells.

THE FEDERAL GAZETTE.

City of Philadelphia.

AT a Meeting of the Corporation, August 28, 1793. called expressly to take into consideration the present alarming state of the city, the Mayor laid before the Board, the following letters and orders, which he had from time to time, issued upon the occasion; and which, at the request of the Corporation, are now laid before the public.

GENTLEMEN,

AS there is great reason to apprehend that a dangerous, infectious disorder now prevails in this city, it is the duty of every department of authority to take the most effectual precautions to prevent its spreading: And as the keeping the streets at this time as clean as possible may conduce to that desirable object, I require that you will immediately upon the receipt of this letter, employ the scavengers in making the streets and gutters in every part of the town as clean as possible, and that as fast as the filth be laid together, that it be *immediately hauled away*.

I recommend that they begin to clean first in Water street, and all the alleys and passages from thence into Front-street, and then proceed to clean the other more airy streets.

I expect that the inhabitants will have the satisfaction of seeing this business going on, this afternoon or to-morrow morning; any delay on your part will reasonably be considered as an improper attention to a very essential duty.

MATTHEW CLARKSON, *Mayor.*

Phila. Aug. 22, 1793.

City Commissioners.

GENTLEMEN,

WHILST the present contagious fever shall continue in this city, it will be proper that every precaution be taken, that can in any degree prevent its spreading; and as it may conduce to that desirable end, I desire that you will be particularly attentive, to cause all the streets, lanes and alleys, in every part of the City, to be kept in a constant state of cleanliness, and to cause the filth and dirt to be hauled away, as speedily as it is heaped together. In executing this duty, you must not confine yourselves to the times prescribed by the ordinance, but cause it to be done as much oftener as may be necessary, to keep them effectually clean. The extra expence attending this business, will be allowed in account.

MATTHEW CLARKSON, *Mayor.*

Philad. Aug. 27. 1793.

FOR THE FEDERAL GAZETTE.

MR. BROWN,

I WISH through the channel of your paper, for the good of the public, to introduce a hint to the Grave-Diggers of this city, to lay every corpse a proper depth under ground; as infectious disorders, are liable to be spread, when they are not above two feet under the earth, which I have reason to believe, has been some times the case.

MONITOR.

Aug. 30.

European Intelligence,

Received by the Ship Adriana, Captain Robertson.

[CONTINUED.]

LONDON, June 24.

Admiralty-Office, June 22, 1793.

Copy of a letter from Captain Edward Pellew, of his Majesty's ship La Nymphe, to Mr. Stephens, dated off Portland, June 19, 1793.

I have the honor to inform you, that, at day-light yesterday morning, I was so fortunate as to fall in with the National French Frigate, La Cleopatra, mounting forty guns, and manned with 320 men, commanded by Monsieur Jean Mullon, three days from St. Maloes, and had taken nothing.

We brought her to close action at half past six, and in fifty-five minutes took possession of her; the two ships having fallen on board each other, we boarded her from the quarter-deck, and struck her colours; and finding it impossible to clear the ships, then hanging head and stern, we came to anchor, which divided us, after we had received on board 150 prisoners. The enemy fought us like brave men, neither ship firing a shot until we had hailed.—Her captain was killed, three lieutenants wounded; the number of men not yet ascertained, but, from the best accounts, about sixty; her mizen-mast overboard, and her tiller shot off.

I am extremely concerned she was not purchased at a less expence of valuable officers and men on our part, whose gallantry I cannot sufficiently regret, and to whose loss I cannot possibly do justice. We had twenty-three men killed, and twenty-seven men wounded, of which a list is enclosed.

I am very particularly indebted to my first lieutenant, Mr. Amherst Morris, and no less so to leiutenants George Luke and Richard Pellew, and I was ably seconded on the quarter-deck by

wards England, during my Mi[illegible] but it is not for these that I cla[illegible] generosity of the English Nation.

"Your Lordship will see that [illegible] necessity alone that made me chan[illegible] name, when I came to seek an a[illegible] in England. I respect the Laws. [illegible] fiction I made use of when at [illegible] was merely local, and I hasten [illegible] pair it by a true declaration of n[illegible]

"If my request can be gra[illegible] will comply with whatever the pru[illegible] of the Minister shall require of m[illegible]

"I have the honour to be, &[illegible]

(Signed) "DUMOURI[illegible]

Lord GRENVILLE's ANSW[illegible]

"*Whitehall, June* 16, 1[illegible]

"I received, Sir, this mornin[illegible] Letter you did me the honour [illegible] dress to me. It is the business [illegible] Secretary of State for the Hon[illegible] partment to take the orders of H[illegible] jesty relative to the residence of [illegible] in this Kingdom, and to notify th[illegible] officially; but as it is to me th[illegible] have addressed yourself on this oc[illegible] I cannot do otherwise than ac[illegible] ledge the receipt of your Lette[illegible] answer the demands which it co[illegible]

"Your stay in England will [illegible] ject to too many inconvenien[illegible] make it possible for the Governm[illegible] this Country to permit it. I can[illegible] regret, that you had not gained [illegible] mation in this particular befo[illegible] came to England. If your wi[illegible] been made known to me befo[illegible] undertook the journey, I woul[illegible] informed you without reserve, [illegible] would have been a useless one. [illegible] mains now with me to point out [illegible] my opinion, that you must co[illegible] without delay, to the decision [illegible] been under the necessity to com[illegible] cate to you by this Letter.

"I have the honour to be, &

(Signed) "GRENVIL[illegible]

M. DUMOURIER.

About the middle of the d[illegible] Thursday last, a dreadful fire bro[illegible] at Stanton St John's, about four [illegible] from Oxford, which entirely de[illegible] twenty-one dwelling-houses, five [illegible] and divers other out buildings, by [illegible] many of the inhabitants are redu[illegible] the utmost distress.

Commercial Failures.

THE malicious and absurd a[illegible] to charge the late commercial [illegible] to the account of the war is p[illegible] exposed in the following obser[illegible] introduced into the fourth edit[illegible] Mr. Bowles's Real Grounds of th[illegible]

"Imported however as the w[illegible] its object, and just in its princi[illegible] most illiberal endeavours are n[illegible] enhance its difficulties, to dep[illegible]

CHAPTER THREE

Church Bells Tolling

From house to house the dread contagion flew,
And on its way a num'rous train hath slew!

—SAMUEL STEARNS, 1793

Sunday, August 25. The spread of the disease and of fear among the citizens had one immediate consequence: people began leaving the city. Clothes were packed in haste, windows slammed and shuttered, doors locked tight. Sometimes servants were ordered to stay behind to guard the house against thieves; sometimes everyone living under a roof fled. Printer and publisher Mathew Carey watched sadly as "almost every hour in the day, carts, waggons, coaches, and chairs, were to be seen transporting families & furniture to the country in every direction."

Hundreds exited Philadelphia on that rainswept Sunday. More left in the days to follow, as Dr. Rush's advice to "Fly from it!" was repeated over and over again. Shop owners, carpenters, councilmen, and printers. Lawyers, ministers, nurses, and bankers. People of every rank and station wanted to escape the spreading pestilence and breathe the fresh, healthy air of the countryside. Twenty-three watchmen were

OPPOSITE: *From* The Federal Gazette, *August 30, 1793.*
(THE LIBRARY COMPANY OF PHILADELPHIA)

Elizabeth Drinker, as she appeared in a silhouette portrait.
(THE HISTORICAL SOCIETY OF PENNSYLVANIA)

---

supposed to patrol the city's streets every night, but their numbers had dwindled to a mere handful by the end of the week.

Suddenly, the fever seemed to be everywhere. Elizabeth Drinker felt surrounded by disease when she made this diary entry for Wednesday, August 28: "There is a man next door but one to us, who Dr. Kuhn says will quickly die of this terrible disorder. Caty Prusia, over against us is very ill, and a man at ye Shoemakers next door to Neighr Waln's; some sick in our Alley."

Mayor Clarkson's order to clean the streets was being carried out, but not very rapidly. Like others around them, many scavengers abandoned their brooms and shovels and ran from the city.

People whispered rumors of more and more deaths. They saw friends and relatives sicken. They heard the church bells tolling, tolling, tolling—and they ran. Drinker's diary entry for August 28 concludes:

"Isaac Wharton and family are moved out of Town, P. Hartshorne's family, and Neighr Waln's also out; the inhabitants are leaving the City in great numbers."

Judge William Lewis saw house after house in his neighborhood abandoned, saw the streets empty, saw the hearses constantly passing his home, and fled. He then wrote a letter to his good friend Dr. Rush, in which he confessed, "I never left Phila. With so much pleasure as yesterday nor never found Such Pleasure in the Country as I do today." Historians now estimate that as many as 20,000 people abandoned the city during the fever.

This meant that thousands were left behind. Most of these stayed because they were poor and had no place to go. They did not own country homes or have relatives or friends outside the city who would be willing to put them up until the fever ended. A few—a very few—chose to stay because they felt a sense of duty to their city and its trapped inhabitants.

One of those who stayed, and would stay throughout the fever, was Matthew Clarkson. He had grown up in a prominent New York family, contributed large sums of money to the Revolutionary cause, helped found the Bank of Pennsylvania, and gone on to amass a fortune as a trustee of the Mutual Company, selling insurance to Philadelphia's citizens. He entered politics as an alderman in 1790, and then because of his record of achievement and an amiable personality, the rest of the aldermen chose him to be mayor in 1792.

Clarkson stayed despite many good reasons to flee. He was sixty years old, with a wife and nine children to look after. In addition, his title of mayor was largely an honorary one. At the time, the mayor of Philadelphia had no real power. All authority to pass laws and raise money was held by a variety of committees made up of members of the town council. Even in an emergency the council was supposed to appoint a committee to determine a course of action.

Add to these one more compelling reason for Clarkson to abandon his post: yellow fever had already seized his wife and killed his youngest son, Gerard.

Mayor Clarkson could have cited his powerlessness, could have pleaded concern for his family, and fled the danger, as many other aldermen were doing. Yet he understood that as mayor he was the sym-

This 1939 painting of Matthew Clarkson was based on a nineteenth-century one and minimizes his most noticeable physical feature. Clarkson suffered from strabismus, a muscle condition that caused his two dark eyes to always peer in different directions.
(THE NATIONAL GRANGE MUTUAL INSURANCE COMPANY/THE GREEN TREE COLLECTION)

bolic head of the town. If he scampered off like the rest, it would be like a father abandoning his family. He chose to stay and act, even though he knew it would mean breaking the law.

One of the first things he did was to ask the country's most prestigious medical society, the College of Physicians, to assemble on that rainy Sunday, August 25. The College was dedicated to improving the science of medicine, and its member physicians were among the best educated and most experienced doctors in the United States. A few had even been around in 1762, when the last yellow fever epidemic had struck. If any medical group was qualified to provide guidance concerning yellow fever, it was the College of Physicians.

What took place that day did not bode well for Clarkson or for Philadelphia. Of the twenty-six physicians who made up the College, only sixteen appeared. Some of those absent had good excuses, such as having to attend to an increasing number of patients ill with the fever. But many physicians had simply chosen not to show up or had already moved to the countryside.

What is more, their meeting produced very little that would calm their fellow citizens. There was a terrible fever running through the city, the learned doctors all readily agreed. But after comparing descriptions of the symptoms, they began to disagree on the nature and cause of the illness as well as what to do about it.

Essentially, the doctors formed two camps. One, headed by Benjamin Rush, believed they were facing yellow fever and that it had a local cause—the stagnant, foul-smelling air that had infested Philadelphia all summer. Some factors affecting the quality of the air, such as the hot, humid, oppressive summer weather, were out of their control. But other things could be done to purify it, such as getting rid of the bad coffee and cleaning up streets and alleyways.

Opposing Dr. Rush was Dr. William Currie. Currie was not as well known as Rush in Philadelphia, but he was the only member of the College who had actually done research on yellow fever—enough to have written two books about the disease. And he wasn't afraid to disagree with his more famous colleague.

Currie agreed that there was a terrible fever infecting the city, but he simply did not think it was yellow fever. In addition, he felt strongly that whatever fever they might be facing had been imported from another area—probably from the West Indies by the recently arrived Santo Domingans—and that it was spread by close contact with an infected person. Currie admitted that the illness was "strengthened by a particular construction of the atmosphere," but he insisted that the best way to deal with it was by quarantining the sick.

Most of the doctors at that first meeting felt they did not know enough about the illness to give it a specific name. While they did not immediately side with Currie, their cautious approach miffed Rush, who felt they should have deferred to his medical opinion. He had, after all, actually dealt with yellow fever firsthand, while Currie had merely studied the disease. Still, Sunday's discussion and disagreements were "a free communication of sentiment," as Dr. Samuel Griffitts remembered. During the weeks to follow, the divide between members of the College would grow wider and the arguments more heated and personal.

The doctors met again on Monday, though this time only eleven of them were in attendance. At this meeting they issued a list of measures for citizens to follow; the list was sent to Mayor Clarkson, who sent it on to Governor Mifflin and the newspapers. Many of the recommendations were intelligent and reasonable: Clean up the streets, set up a hospital for fever victims, avoid fatigue, limit the intake of beer and wine, put patients in airy rooms, and remove fouled clothes and bed linens frequently. Other suggestions offered a false sense of security: The doctors recommended that strong-smelling substances, such as vinegar, be sprinkled on handkerchiefs and held to the nose to ward off the fever, and that gunpowder be burned to purify the air.

One suggestion alarmed many citizens: Stay away from anyone with the fever. Heightening the panic was what the list did not offer: A cure for the disease.

When the list was published on Tuesday, the blazing sun had reappeared, and fetid, warm air once again choked the city. And people were still pulling out of Philadelphia in droves. Even those who were initially hesitant about leaving read the list and joined the exodus.

Philadelphia that day was a completely changed place from the week before. Few people walked on the streets who were not fleeing. Those who felt they had to go out to check on an aged parent, or to buy medicine or food, did so wearing vinegar-soaked clothing and clutching bags of camphor—a bitter-smelling substance we now use in insect repellent—to their noses. Mathew Carey went around town noting carefully what was happening and would later turn these observations into a written history of the epidemic. "The smoke of tobacco," he pointed out, "being regarded as a preventative, many persons, even women and small boys, had segars almost constantly in their mouths. Others placing full confidence in garlic, chewed it almost the whole day; some kept it in their pockets and shoes."

Everyone walked in the middle of the street so they wouldn't get too close to infected homes. People stayed clear of funerals, doctors, and ministers. "Acquaintances and friends avoided each other in the streets," Carey observed, "and only signified their regard by a cold nod."

Stores and workshops began to close. Every school in town suddenly shut its doors, either because the teachers demanded it or because no students showed up for classes. Fires were lit on street corners to dry up the unhealthy, humid air and to drive away the bad smells; the sound

Four men in a tavern extol the fine quality of Isaac Jones's tobacco in this early watercolor advertisement. (The Library Company of Philadelphia)

of gunfire erupted day and night as frightened citizens attempted to cleanse the air with gunpowder smoke. "The streets," Carey reported, "wore the appearance of gloom and melancholy."

There were, of course, a few hardy individuals out and about. A contributor to *Dunlap's American Daily Advertiser* who went by the initials "A. B." could be seen poking around rainwater barrels in his neighborhood. "Whoever will take the trouble to examine [them]," he noted, "will find millions of the mosquitoes fishing about the water with great agility, in a state not quite prepared to emerge and fly off." "A. B." then advised readers that a gill (about four ounces) of common oil poured into the water would kill off these troublesome creatures within twenty-four hours.

Most people weren't interested in doing household experiments and instead played it safe by hiding indoors. They kept busy, however. Day after day was spent scrubbing floors, walls, and ceilings. Rooms were whitewashed and then sprinkled with vinegar. Logs burned day and night in fireplaces despite the oppressive heat, and gunpowder and other noxious chemicals were tossed in frequently.

Charles Willson Peale, noted painter, inventor, and collector of natural history objects, shut himself, his wife Betsy, and six of his children inside his large museum-residence. He spent a great deal of time classifying his mineral collection, though he made certain "the house is fumed with Vinegar" and that he performed "about 6 firing of a [musket] within the House" every day. The live birds he had collected as specimens were cooked and eaten, eliminating the need to go to the market.

All went well until Betsy ventured into the garden and, according to Peale, smelled something disagreeable. The next day she fell ill and was confined to bed. Their family doctor had already died of the fever, and his replacement soon caught it also. After this, Peale took over the doctoring chores himself even though he too eventually contracted a mild case of yellow fever. Both would survive, though they never got over the fear these near escapes caused and kept their doors securely bolted against all visitors throughout the plague.

Dr. Benjamin Duffield, a member of the College of Physicians, had his own recommendation for dealing with the fever, which he gladly published in the newspapers for all to read. Fresh dirt should be strewn around every room to a depth of two inches, he wrote, and that dirt should be changed every day. For additional protection, he suggested taking frequent warm baths and inhaling finely ground black pepper.

Ordinary citizens also offered advice and preventives through the town's newspapers. One writer who signed his name "A Hint" said the

Like many people in Philadelphia, Charles Willson Peale decided to lock himself and his family inside their house in an attempt to avoid the fever.

(THE LIBRARY COMPANY OF PHILADELPHIA)

---

cause of the fever was the stinking barrels of rotting garbage routinely found in backyards and basements. He suggested that instead of storing garbage in these containers, the "bones, with some flesh on them, the entrails of poultry, and many other corruptive matters" should be tossed into the street "where the dogs would devour the meat, and the cows the vegetables."

"W. F." warned everyone to prepare carefully before venturing out of doors and suggested that "Vinegar of the Four Thieves" be used liberally. For the uneducated, "W. F." provided a detailed recipe: "Take of Rue, Wormwood and Lavender, of each one handful; put these altogether with a gallon of the best vinegar into a stone pan . . . and let them stand within the warmth of a fire, to infuse for eight days." This brew was to be combined in quart bottles with three-quarters of an ounce of camphor. Next the reader—assuming he or she has not contracted the disease during the long cooking process—should "rub the temples and loins with this preparation . . . wash the mouth, and snuff up some of it into the nostrils." "W. F." was confident that anyone who followed this procedure could wander about town in complete safety.

Midwives, nurses, dentists, barbers, apothecaries, wandering healers, quack physicians, and next-door neighbors offered opinions on the disease, too. Ads appeared in the newspapers hawking Peruvian bark, salt of vinegar, refined camphor, and other concoctions, such as Daffey's Elixir (which contained so much pure alcohol that a glass of it could put a person into a drunken stupor). The science of medicine at the end of the eighteenth century still relied a great deal on ancient myths and folk remedies. Because of this, people did not automatically reject the opinion of someone simply because that person wasn't a trained doctor.

Despite all the helpful suggestions offered, people continued to die. Twenty-two on Wednesday; twenty-four on Thursday; twenty on Friday. Benjamin Rush took time out of a busy day to write his wife. He told her about his dead and dying patients, and about the neighbors who had abandoned their homes and businesses. "Our neighborhood will be desolate in a day or two," he concluded solemnly.

During times of plague, quack doctors always appeared to sell their "cures" to frightened citizens. This mid-eighteenth-century engraving shows one hawking his medicines to villagers in northern Europe. (THE COLLEGE OF PHYSICIANS OF PHILADELPHIA)

Philadelphia was a city in panic and flight. It did not even help when Mayor Clarkson acted on another recommendation from the College of Physicians. The tolling bells that had so thoroughly terrified everyone were ordered to remain still. The great silence that followed did little to comfort those left behind. It was too much like the eternal silence of the grave.

of nitre are insignificant. A sea-
agement has been known to entirely
nguish the yellow fever infection
board of ships,—The following re-
ities to preserve from infection are
n the first authority—cleanliness,
erfulness, courage, regular and tem-
ate living; with the very moderate
of brandy and other liquors, so far
o act as a gentle stimulus upon the
its. Soaking sheets of paper in
issolution of salt-petre, und agita-
g the sheets, thus soaked, through a
m, is also an excellent preservative
m all infection. *(Nat. Gaz.)*

—

Died, on the 9th inst. at his seat near
right's Ferry, on the Susquehanna,
Hon. *William Augustus Atlee*, Esq.
esident of the courts of common pleas
West-Chester, Lancaster, York, and
uphin Counties.

Y THIS DAY'S MAIL.

NEW-YORK, September 13.

tract of a letter from Capt. Thomas Grives, late commander of the Ship Neptune, of Pool, bound from this port to Newfoundland, to a Gentleman in this city, dated Boston 8th September, 1793.

"I take the first opportunity of in-
ming you, that on Sunday 1st inst.
lat. 42, 43, long. 64. I was taken by
e French privateer Marseilles, after
ing chased from nine in the morning
ten o'clock at night, during the
ase the privateer fired her bow-guns,
18 pounders. When night came on
ost sight of the privateer, I then fixed
ight on a pork barrel, dropped it over-
ard, fired a swivel, and altered my
urse four points; the privateer steered
r the light, and all hands on board of
r were prepared for action, but on
ding the deception, I was again espid
the assistance of night glasses which
d been taken out of a British vessel
hich the Marseilles had captured—
hased, taken and am now a prisoner
ere."

—

We are informed, there will be a
eeting of the Citizens this evening,
the Tontine Coffee-House, to consi-
er of the best means of preventing the
troduction of the alarming disease,
at now ravages Philadelphia.

xtract of two letters from a gentleman in Philadelphia, to his friend in this city.

September 10.

"Our neighbourhood is as yet very
ealthy, several have been cured of the
ver, which proves that its violence is
bating, new cases are not so frequent
at first. Secretary Hamilton and his

Resolved, That the said committee do advertise in the public newspapers the proposed meeting.

Arrived—Ship Providence, Jenkins, West-Indies; Sloop Betsey, Chappell, New-London; Apollo, Anderson, New-port; Friendship, Johnston, Baltimore.

FOR THE FEDERAL GAZETTE.

MR. BROWN,

IF Dr. Kuhn had been *practically* acquainted with the yellow fever, he would have known, that it often puts on all the intermediate stages between a mild bilious remitting, and a violent inflammatory or putrid fever.

Had he, moreover consulted the writings of Dr. Sydenham, and attended more closely to the diseases of his own country, he would have known, that no two epidemics of unequal force, can exist long together. The common bilious remittent, yielded to the ruthless and solitary despotism of the prevailing epidemic, on the 5th of the present month. Dr. Rush has seen no fever since that day, that was not accompanied by a red, or yellow eye.

If Dr. Kuhn looks for a yellow colour on the skin of Dr. Rush's patients who have recovered; to convince him that they have been cured of a yellow, instead of a common bilious fever, he will be disappointed. The great advantage of the mode of cure adopted by Dr. Rush, consists, in its *preventing*, not in curing a *yellow* fever. The yellowness on the skin, occurs, (with a few exceptions) in such patients only as have been neglected in the beginning of the disorder, or who have recovered in spite of the use of Dr. Kuhn's remedies.

Dr. Kuhn will do a great kindness to the public, by keeping his opinions to himself, in the present distressing juncture, and not add to the mortality of the disorder, and the calamities of the city, by publications, which serve only to mislead some practitioners, and to lessen the confidence of some of the citizens in the only remedies which are safe, practicable, and successful, (in ninety-nine cases of an hundred) in the present epidemic.

Sept. 13th.

For the Better Protec-
tion of the City.

WHEREAS, the City Commissioners
have observed, a great number of dwel-
ling houses and stores in this City, which
for the present, are shut up, and havin
good reason to apprehend, that som
evil disposed persons, may avail them
selves of the opportunity, to commi
Burglaries, or other outrages,—The sai
Commissioners, taking the same unde
their serious consideration, have agreed
that a number of able bodied men, wel
recommended for their *Sobriety, Honest*
and Vigilance, shall be employed in ad
dition to the present Watch, to act as
Patrol, or in such other manner, as th
said Commissioners shall think most ex
pedient; for the more effectual protec
tion of the Lives and properties of th
Citizens, for the time being.

NOW, this public notice is hereb
given, to any person, or persons, willin
to execute the trust, being recommend
ed as aforesaid, that they may make ap
plication to either of the Commissioner
without delay, or at their stated meet
ings, on Tuesday, and Friday evening
at the Court-House—They being dete
mined, to proceed therein, with a
possible, prudent, dispatch.

By Order of the Board,
JOHN MEASE, *Clerk.*

Sept. 13, 1793.

The several Printers in the City, are re quested, to publish the above, in their New papers. d2t.

To the Citizens.

A SUPPLY of old shirts, shifts an
linen, of any kind, is much wanted a
the Hospital, for the sick.

Those who have any to spare, ar
requested, to send them to the State
House, where a person is appointed t
receive them.

MATTHEW CLARKSON, *Mayor*

Sept. 13, 1793.

The Printers are requested, to publis
this Advertisement, for a few days.

To the Citizens.

Those who have been intrusted wit
the care of the houses belonging to citi
zens who have removed into the coun
try, are requested to send the Fir
Buckets belonging to such families, t
the Court-House, where they will b
placed under the care of the Constab
of the watch, and be ready for use i
case of fire.

This precaution at this time, is ex
tremely necessary, and it is hoped, tha
it will be particularly attended to.

MATTHEW CLARKSON, *Mayor*

Sept. 12, 1793.

The Printers of newspapers in th

CHAPTER FOUR

Confusion, Distress, and Utter Desolation

In fact, government of every kind was almost wholly vacated.

—Mathew Carey, November 1793

Friday, August 30. The deathly quiet of this Friday morning was shattered by the sharp, echoing boom of a cannon. Several minutes went by, and then another boom rattled windows and shook houses in the city. Under orders from Mayor Clarkson, a militia company from nearby Fort Mifflin was hauling a small cannon along the streets of Philadelphia, stopping every few yards to fire off another blast.

Actually, the cannon wasn't Clarkson's idea. Governor Mifflin and the state legislature had sent him an urgent note insisting that "gunpowder, and other salutory preparations, be flashed through the streets" as the College of Physicians had suggested.

Clarkson did not think these "salutory preparations" would do much more than scare citizens, but he knew the legislature and the governor were in a panic. On August 27 a much depleted and very nervous Pennsylvania legislature (only ten of eighteen senators and thirty-six of

Opposite: *From* The Federal Gazette, *September 14, 1793.*
(The Library Company of Philadelphia)

seventy-two representatives) had arrived at the state house to begin their work. Two days later unease turned to fear when they discovered that something terrible had taken place during the night. Their young doorkeeper, Joseph Fry, had died in his bed of the fever.

Fry's rooms were in the west wing of the building, not very far from where the senators and representatives met. One reason they had assembled was to find a way to reassure the citizens of Pennsylvania about the fever, but the fact that the fever had entered their building—that Fry had breathed the same air they were breathing now—unsettled them.

The speaker of the senate, Samuel Powel, sought to reassure his fellow legislators by getting Dr. Rush's advice on how to avoid the disease. "If you can enable me to allay [their concerns]," Powel told his friend, then "the public Business will probably proceed." Rush was so busy tending patients that he could only scribble on the back of Powel's note, "I know of but one certain preventative of the disorder, & that is to keep at a distance from infected persons and places."

This was not comforting news to the governor or the forty-six other men crowded into the state house. In the days that followed, the two houses, with the urgings of the governor, rushed through a series of hastily written resolutions. One recommended improvements to the public health office, while another suggested that the fever had been imported from the West Indies by French immigrants. They also rammed through a quarantine act. Then the state legislature handed over all emergency powers to the governor and adjourned until December. As Assemblyman Jacob Hiltzheimer noted in his diary, "The members decline remaining in the city."

The governor then turned the entire problem over to Mayor Clarkson, directing him to halt ships from the West Indies for inspection and to do everything possible "to allay the public inquietude, and effectually remove its cause." He did not tell Clarkson how he was to do any of this and did not grant him any special emergency powers or funds.

A front view of the state house and Congress Hall prior to the outbreak of yellow fever.
(THE HISTORICAL SOCIETY OF PENNSYLVANIA)

The next day, Governor Mifflin claimed he wasn't feeling well and headed for his country home far from the fouled air of the state house. In effect, the government of Pennsylvania had closed its doors as tightly as any of Philadelphia's shopkeepers had.

Mayor Clarkson, meanwhile, faced mounting problems. The mayor showed up at city hall every day to learn what new crisis had developed, meet visitors, and consider options. But there was little he could do. Every day more and more city officials failed to show up at work: judges and clerks, aldermen and secretaries.

Orders had been issued to clean up the streets and patrol the wharves, but few people were around to carry out such orders. One day thirty ships arrived, thirteen of them from the West Indies, but no one was available to stop them from docking or discharging passengers. The bodies of the indigent dead were carted to the potter's field and dumped, but no gravediggers were there to bury them.

Mayor Clarkson's greatest concern was the mounting number of penniless people in Philadelphia. As well-off citizens closed their businesses and fled the city, they left behind thousands of individuals without any source of income. When these people became ill, they had no money to pay for food, medicine, a physician, or a nurse.

The city almshouse on Spruce Street was jammed with over three hundred paupers, while private institutions, such as the Friends' Alms House, were also filled to capacity. Desperately ill paupers were wandering the streets, or abandoned in their homes with no one to care for them. Even the Pennsylvania Hospital barred fever victims, because it feared that the crowded condition of its building would allow the disease to spread wildly.

Adding to Philadelphia's woes was a new problem. Many nearby farmers were refusing to bring food into the diseased city; the little food that did make it to market was extremely expensive, sometimes costing two or three times as much as it had before the fever struck.

Soon after Mayor Clarkson heard Rush's news that yellow fever had reappeared, he tried to address the problem of indigent individuals. He summoned the "Overseers and Guardians of the Poor," the only official group then dealing with the poor of Philadelphia and surrounding areas. Six Overseers managed the almshouse and were responsible for what went on inside that building, while fourteen Guardians took care of those in need outside the almshouse.

The situation was grave, Clarkson told the Overseers and Guardians. Sick paupers had to be gotten off the streets and out of the alleyways. Not only did they frighten those who came upon them, but they might very well be spreading the disease.

The Guardians left the meeting resolved to act, but the results demonstrated how completely disorganized the city had become. The Guardians went immediately to Ricketts' Circus at Twelfth Street and High and seized the building. Until John Bill Ricketts had taken his show to Manhattan for the summer, his circus had been one of the city's most celebrated entertainment spots and the showplace for his equestrian talents. Latin teacher James Hardie described Ricketts' Circus as "a place to dispel the gloom of the thoughtful, exercise the lively activity of the young and gay, or to relax the minds of the sedentary or industrious trader."

Seven sick persons were scooped up from the streets and deposited at Ricketts'. The only trouble was that no one could be found to care for them. The sick lay in the stiflingly hot building unattended, calling out for water, moaning pitifully, and vomiting on themselves. Mathew Carey took up the story: "Of these, one crawled out on the commons, where he died. . . . Two died in the circus." Two bodies were removed, but "the other lay in a state of putrefaction for above forty eight hours."

Ricketts' was located in a quiet residential area many blocks away from the docks where the pestilence had first struck. The pitiful sounds

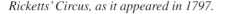

Ricketts' Circus, as it appeared in 1797. (THE LIBRARY COMPANY OF PHILADELPHIA)

coming from the circus and the sight of dead fever victims did not exactly "dispel the gloom" of the households nearby. They demanded that the sick be moved and the corpse be disposed of properly—and they threatened to burn the place down if action wasn't taken quickly.

The Guardians sent a hauler to remove the foul body, but the driver couldn't get it into the coffin by himself. A brave servant girl noticed the man's trouble and, Carey continued, "offered her services, provided he would not inform the family with whom she lived (else she would be at once dismissed). She accordingly helped him put the body into the coffin, which was by then crawling with maggots, and in such a state as to be ready to fall in pieces."

Ricketts' was clearly not the best place to care for seriously ill patients, so the Guardians decided to find a building in a more isolated area. They chose a large, unoccupied mansion called Bush Hill, located on a rolling hill about two and a half miles northwest of the city.

Neither Mayor Clarkson nor the Guardians had the legal right to take control of Bush Hill. But the owner, William Hamilton, was living in England at the time, and his caretaker, Thomas Boyles, could do little to stop them. Those still alive at Ricketts' were moved to Bush Hill, and other desperately ill people followed. All eleven rooms, plus the hallways and staircase landings, were quickly jammed full.

Four doctors were chosen to care for these patients. Two of them became ill shortly after being appointed, while the sickness in the city consumed the time of the other two. They did show up at Bush Hill every so often, but they never established a regular schedule for visits.

Meanwhile, volunteers were called to help at Bush Hill, but only one responded, a second-year medical student named Charles Caldwell. He found conditions at Bush Hill "limited, crude and insufficient." The place had been taken over so hastily and with so little attention to medical needs that it was "a likeness in miniature of the city at the time, a scene of deep confusion and distress, not to say of utter desolation."

This engraving of Bush Hill was done in 1793 to accompany an article about William Hamilton that appeared in New York Magazine. (THE LIBRARY COMPANY OF PHILADELPHIA)

And then the situation got even worse. "Shortly after this," Carey wrote, "the guardians of the poor for the city . . . ceased the performance of their duties; nearly the whole of them having removed out of the city." Only three remained to see to the mounting problems in Philadelphia and to administer Bush Hill. Of the three who stayed, two died of the fever, while the other became too sick to do any sort of work.

As all this was taking place, deaths in the city increased, from nineteen on September 1 to forty-two on September 8. Whole families were swept away in a matter of days. David Flickwir and five members of his family perished, as did Samuel Weatherby and his wife and their four children. Godfrey Gebler lost eleven family members. Many of these people died, Carey pointed out, "without a human being to hand them a drink of water, to administer medicines, or to perform any charitable office for them."

Every morning found bodies lying in the streets. Every day a new horror story surfaced. Carey told of a pregnant woman who went into labor even while "her husband and two children lay dead in the same room with her." No midwife attended her, and no relative or neighbor gave her comfort. She managed to crawl to a window and get a passerby's attention. "With his assistance, she was delivered of the child, which died in a few minutes, as did the mother."

By the end of the first week of September, the yellow fever epidemic had driven the state government from Philadelphia and crippled the city's administration. It then struck at the federal government with a vengeance. Secretary of the Treasury Alexander Hamilton and his wife fell ill with the fever on September 5, and left the city. Six clerks of the Treasury Department also contracted the disease, leaving just one, Joshua Dawson, at his post.

Attorney General Edmund Randolph was away negotiating an Indian treaty, and his department fell into disarray almost immediately. The post office ceased doing business when three of its clerks grew ill. Thomas Jefferson, meanwhile, had submitted his resignation (which was to take effect on December 31) because of Washington's neutrality policy and went home to his estate in Virginia. Nearly everyone, Washington observed with consternation and annoyance, had "matters of private concernment which required them to be absent."

The president recognized the mortal danger federal employees faced and urged department heads to move their offices from Philadelphia to Germantown, some five miles away. A few days later Washington himself began preparing to leave for Virginia.

"It was my wish to have continued [in Philadelphia] longer," he wrote to his personal secretary, Tobias Lear, "but as Mrs. Washington was unwilling to leave me surrounded by the malignant fever wch. Prevailed, I could not think of hazarding her . . . any longer by *my* continuing in the City the house in which we lived being, in a manner, blockaded, by the disorder and was becoming every day more and more fatal."

On the morning of September 10, George and Martha Washington

No contemporary illustrations of Philadelphia's yellow fever epidemic exist, but scenes similar to this one from a cholera epidemic in France must have been very common in Philadelphia in 1793.

(THE PHILADELPHIA MUSEUM OF ART/THE WILLIAM H. HELFAND COLLECTION) headed south toward Mount Vernon. He planned to be away from the seat of the federal government for fifteen days or so and did not take any official papers with him. In the weeks ahead, he would postpone his return several times, as reports reached him that the epidemic was growing worse.

Without realizing it, the president set a constitutional crisis in motion when he exited the city. Many people, Thomas Jefferson and future president James Madison included, felt that Washington could not legally convene Congress anywhere but within the city limits of Philadelphia. Without Congress to pass laws and appropriate money, the workings of the federal government would eventually come to a grinding halt.

Robert Morris lent George Washington his smaller home (on the left) while the federal government was situated in Philadelphia. (THE LIBRARY COMPANY OF PHILADELPHIA)

Two days after the president left, and even before he reached his Virginia home, a meteorite fell out of the morning sky and thudded into Third Street. In a city that was fast falling apart, it was seen as an omen that even worse things were yet to come.

for this excellent phyſician
I ſhould withhold my obſer-
rts of his paper.
the ſymptoms of the fever,
ends for an adult ten grains of
grains of jalap for a doſe, to
ſix hours, 'till four or five
are produced. I venture to
d muſt obſerve, if the patient
coſtive it will be better not
ere be occaſion for an evacu-
more adviſable, and only one
hich nature directs; nor ought
except in particular caſes. In
, which rapidly exhauſts the
prefer an injection,* which
caſionally. Diarhæa, and too
ns, muſt be particularly at-
ſters of ſtarch, with from 20
lanum, muſt be injected after
peating them 2 or 3 times a
d uſing the proper aſtringents

is violently affected in the be-
caſe, relief may be frequently
; the feet in luke-warm water
hour; this refreſhes, and af-
dry, by getting immediately
ing a little wine whey, a gen-
enerally produced. It would
ck this ſuddenly, but, if it be-
would alſo be improper to
e patients ſink very faſt.
recommends the loſs of 8 or
d, "if the pulſe be full or
the tenſion or fulneſs of the
ue."—I really cannot agree
this reduction of force, for as
, languor and proſtration of
ſucceed the firſt or apparently
, that too much attention
the ſupport of the drooping
ooling teas, and drinks, which
mends in addition to the pur-
and conſtantly keeping the
ooling phyſic, it appears that
tion is to reduce the violence
fter this "if the pulſe ſhould
low" he recommends ſeveral
fficacious remedies, but only
ſſion of the ſever. It muſt be
metimes there is no entire in-
indications as denote what are
fevers; and if this were al-
might lead to a dangerous ſu-
ho attend the ſick. This was
ce, but it has been found by
ce, that in intermitting fevers,
nt medicines have been given
ll the ſtates, without waiting
n. A ſimilar practice prevails
fevers. Bliſters in the laſt
rder, the doctor recommends
ty, for nothing elſe will raiſe
natoſe ſtate nto which they
ſo cloſely the antiphlogiſtic
tion to the bliſters we may uſe
tard to the ſoles of the feet

equently accompanied by ſuch
tomach is difficultly brought to
dminiſtered. Camomile tea
, not only to cleanſe it, but to
emetics ought to be given, as
diminiſh the ſtrength. Cor-
ith a few drops of laudanum

To the Citizens.

THE perſons who are employed to remove the dead, have been frequently interrupted, inſulted and threatned, whilſt performing their buſineſs, by perſons who appear to poſſeſs no ſentiments of humanity, but ſuch as particularly concern themſelves.

In order therefore to prevent ſuch conduct in future, NOTICE is hereby given, that proſecutions will be inſtituted againſt all thoſe who ſhall offend herein.

The public ſafety requires that protection be given to thoſe uſeful perſons, and the good citizens are called upon to afford it to them, and to point out to the legal authority, all thoſe who ſhall moleſt them in their employment.

MATTHEW CLARKSON, *Mayor.*
Sept. 17. 1793.

To the Citizens.

Thoſe who have been intruſted with the care of the houſes belonging to citizens who have removed into the country, are requeſted to ſend the Fire Buckets belonging to ſuch families, to the Court-Houſe, where they will be placed under the care of the Conſtable of the watch, and be ready for uſe in caſe of fire.

This precaution at this time, is extremely neceſſary, and it is hoped, that it will be particularly attended to.

MATTHEW CLARKSON, *Mayor.*
Sept. 12, 1793.

The Printers of newſpapers in the city, are requeſted to inſert the above.

To the Citizens.

A SUPPLY of old ſhirts, ſhifts and linen, of any kind, is much wanted at the Hoſpital, for the ſick.

Thoſe who have any to ſpare, are requeſted, to ſend them to the State-Houſe, where a perſon is appointed to receive them.

MATTHEW CLARKSON, *Mayor.*
Sept. 13, 1793.

The Printers are requeſted, to publiſh this Advertiſement, for a few days.

☞ The great want of Buckets at the recent Fire in Second ſtreet, induces a citizen to ſuggeſt to ſuch of the inhabitants as ſhut up their houſes on leaving the City, the evident Propriety of depoſiting their Fire Buckets &c. in ſome Public Building, or elſewhere,

Mr. BROWN,

I HAVE juſt now ſeen a note in Bache's paper, mentioning that contagion had reached the Jail. have juſt returned from it; and I dismiſſed two vagrants to the Hoſ at Buſh-Hill, that appeared ſuſpici But I can aſſure my fellow-citizens, it is not there, nor is there any o kind of ſever in the houſe, which i markably healthy, only one death ing taken place in the l ſt, fi months, and that, by confluent S Pox.

It would perhaps be prudent for magiſtrates to commit no vagrant they can conſiſtent with their d avoid it. If they are only guilty ſleeping out in the open air, or any vial miſdemeanor, it would be bette excuſe it, than run the riſk of en dering the moſt fertile ſource of ſe contagion, that could poſſibly exi this city.

B. DUFFIELL
Thurſday, 10. A. M.

CHAPTER FIVE

"It Was Our Duty"

The Lord was pleased to strengthen us, and remove all fear from us, and disposed our hearts to be as useful as possible.

—ABSALOM JONES AND RICHARD ALLEN, JANUARY 1794

Thursday, September 5. It was clear that the fever was winning. People were still streaming from the city in droves; houses, businesses, and shops were closed and dark; the sick, dying, and dead were everywhere to be seen. Amid all this a remarkable meeting took place at the Free African Society on Fifth Street, just south of Walnut.

The Free African Society was founded in 1787, the first organization in America created by blacks for blacks. Its purpose was to help members who were destitute and to provide care for widows and fatherless children. On that Thursday the elders of the society assembled to consider something extraordinary: Would they use their association members and their skills to help their struggling white neighbors?

A few days before, a letter had arrived from Benjamin Rush urging the society to help nurse the sick and attend to the dead. One reason they should come forward, Rush contended, was that God had seen fit to grant blacks a special resistance to the dreaded disease.

OPPOSITE: *From* The Federal Gazette, *September 19, 1793.*
(THE LIBRARY COMPANY OF PHILADELPHIA)

In reality, this wasn't true. A small number of blacks who had grown up in either Africa or the West Indies had had the disease as children and survived. Through this encounter with the fever their blood automatically produced antibodies that either fought off the yellow fever virus entirely or reduced its impact on the individual significantly. Most blacks in Philadelphia didn't have this natural immunity and would suffer the ravages of the fever along with whites. But early in September the vast majority of sufferers Rush saw and heard about were white. Rush truly believed what he told the elders.

Most of those gathered at the meeting had been slaves at one time and knew how oppressive some of the whites around them could be. And while Philadelphia had approximately 3,000 free blacks, there were still over 200 blacks being kept as slaves. They were also well aware that the opportunities routinely granted to white citizens—to rise in business and politics—were still being denied them. In 1793 over 50 percent of Philadelphia's blacks were live-in domestic workers, doing the cooking, cleaning, laundering, and child caring for better-off whites.

This August advertisement for a runaway slave was just one of many reminders to free blacks in Philadelphia that their status in the United States was still quite precarious.

(THE LIBRARY COMPANY OF PHILADELPHIA)

Six Dollars Reward.

RAN AWAY, on the 12th inſtant, a Sambo Boy, called ALEXANDER, comonly pronounced Ellick, a native of Jamaica, about 20 years old, pock-marked, 5 feet 3 or 4 inches high, ſlim made, ſtamped on the breaſt with the letters I F C / P P x ſpeaks very good French, and lately arrived from Cape Francois, where he lived ſeveral years, had on when he ran away a pair of new ſhoes with plated buckles, a new pair of nankeen trowſers, a ſtriped blue, red and white jacket, looks ſmart and active. Whoever apprehends ſaid boy, or ſecures him in gaol, ſo that his maſter may get him again, ſhall have the above reward, by applying to the Printer hereof.

Aug. 17. d4t

Absalom Jones gazes out resolutely in this 1810 portrait done by Charles Willson Peale's son Raphaelle. (The Delaware Art Museum, gift of the Absalom Jones School)

Every one of them had suffered in one way or another at the hands of whites, some of them in appalling ways. Two of the elders, Absalom Jones and Richard Allen, had once been worshipers at St. George Methodist Church, a congregation composed of both whites and blacks. The blacks had actually helped erect the church building, and Allen was a preacher popular among all members.

Then one day as Jones knelt in prayer at the altar, white trustees grabbed him and ordered him to sit in the back of the church. Jones was a large man and strong enough to shake off his attackers, but he did not respond to his mishandling with force of his own. In a calm voice, he told the trustees, "Wait until the prayer is over, and I will trouble you no more." Black parishioners then walked out of St. George's, and Jones and Allen each established a separate church of his own.

As recently as that very summer they had been shown their position in the Philadelphia society that was now pleading for their help. Several black leaders had attempted to raise $3,000 in order to build a new church, only to discover that few whites were willing to contribute. But when the refugees from Santo Domingo began arriving, those same people were eager to hand over more than $15,000 in donations for the new arrivals' relief. Adding to the insult was the fact that many of these refugees had brought along their own slaves.

If any group of individuals had reason to ignore the sufferings of their neighbors, the elders of the Free African Society certainly did. Yet they did not hesitate. They were, as Jones and Allen would write later, "sensible that it was our duty to do all the good we could to our fellow mortals."

The elders went out that very day in pairs, visiting houses around the city. Jones and Allen went together and immediately discovered a house in tiny Emsley's Alley where the mother was already dead, the father was dying, and two small children huddled together, frightened and hungry. They sent word to city hall and then went to another and another and another house. "We visited upwards of twenty families that day," they recalled. "They were scenes of woe indeed!"

Volunteers from the Free African Society were the first to enter the homes of most fever victims. What they saw was burned forever into their memories. "Many whose friends, and relations had left them," Jones and Allen said, "died unseen, and unassisted. We . . . found them in various situations, some laying on the floor, as bloody as if they had been dipt in it, without any appearance of their having had, even a drink of water for their relief; others laying on a bed with their clothes on, as if they had come in fatigued, and lain down to rest; some appeared, as if they had fallen down dead on the floor."

The next day, Jones and Allen went to Mayor Clarkson to ask how their group could be of help. To say that Clarkson was grateful for their aid is an understatement; everyone else the mayor had counted on to help battle the spreading fever—leaders in the business community, church groups, elected representatives, and civil servants—had fled in terror. The Free African Society was the one and only group to step forward and offer its services.

After this, whenever anyone requested help, the society sent a volunteer as quickly as possible. No set fee was charged for their services, which might include nursing the individual, cleaning up the sickroom, washing clothes and linens, going out to buy food and medicine, and caring for other family members. If an individual could afford to pay a dollar or two for a full day's care, the money was accepted. But since the people they helped were usually poor, the black nurses often stayed and helped a person for no money at all.

Within a few days, a problem developed. Demand for in-house care far exceeded the number of nurses available. Neighbors who could afford it soon began bidding against each other for the services of available nurses, until there were times when a nurse's fee would reach four or five dollars a day. This was a great deal of money when you consider that the average yearly income in Philadelphia then was around $200.

Virtually everyone supplying goods and services to the city had raised their rates, explaining that shortages of items and the general danger forced up their costs. Yet it was only the black nurses who were openly criticized. This anger eventually led to black nurses being abused verbally in the streets, and, in a few cases, male nurses were attacked physically.

These complaints made their way to Clarkson, though he was misled to believe that the black nurses were going about town demanding

Some chimney sweeps and a yapping dog have gathered around a young woman who has dropped her pie on Lombard Street. Lombard Street was located in South Philadelphia and was the main artery of the Cedar Ward black community at the end of the eighteenth century. (THE HISTORICAL SOCIETY OF PENNSYLVANIA)

exorbitant rates for their work. It was only when he met with Jones and Allen to discuss the situation that he learned it was the white citizens who were bidding up the prices.

The mayor knew he couldn't order black nurses to refuse any fee over a dollar. If he forced them to hold down their costs, he would have to do the same with every merchant, laborer, and farmer doing business in town. How much food would be brought to market if he insisted that only preplague prices be charged? How many carters would haul away diseased corpses? What was happening with the black nurses was a classic example of demand exceeding supply, resulting in higher prices, and nothing more. So Clarkson immediately issued a statement expressing his complete support for the efforts of the society. He also had an ad published in the newspapers that admonished citizens to cease bothering the black nurses as they went about town to their work.

Once this controversy was put aside, members of the Free African Society patrolled the streets daily, rounding up the ill and finding shelter for homeless children. If word came to them that a fever victim was shut up at home without anyone to care for him or her, Jones and Allen sent a representative to investigate. The most seriously ill were taken by cart to Bush Hill; the dead were placed in coffins and hauled to the graveyards.

To do this sort of work, Jones and Allen had to mobilize an army of helpers. Exactly how many blacks were involved in the relief effort is not known. They stepped forward to save lives and relieve suffering, and did so without thought of receiving individual acclaim. We know that Jones and Allen were in direct contact with approximately three hundred blacks and that there were far more black nurses (both male and female) than white nurses.

The names of most of these nurses have been lost to history. In their book Jones and Allen mention William Gray, who organized and supervised the burying of the dead, and Cyrus Bustill, who helped recruit volunteers, as well as Sampson, Sarah Bass, Mary Scott, and Caesar Cranchal. Named and unnamed, they were noticed moving about the city, performing the tasks other shunned.

The vomit that yellow fever patients spewed forth, as well as the blood and offensive odors, were particular horrors to most people, even those medically trained. Young Dr. Isaac Cathrall found these bodily discharges disgusting: "The matter ejected [from the stomach] was of a dark color, resembling coffee grounds, sometimes mixed with blood; great flatulency; haemorrhages from different parts of the body; tongue frequently covered over with blood . . . ; urine very offensive."

Not only were these evacuations and odors loathsome, they were considered dangerous. Dr. Cathrall knew a nurse "who I am almost certain received the infection from a patient . . . for the matter thrown up by vomiting emitted a peculiarly foetid smell, which affected her soon after she had carried it out of the room."

Dr. Cathrall flatly refused to touch the vomit of a patient for any reason, as did most other people; the black nurses, however, had no choice. Their job, after all, was to care for and clean up the patients.

Twenty-one-year-old Isaac Heston was quick to appreciate the work

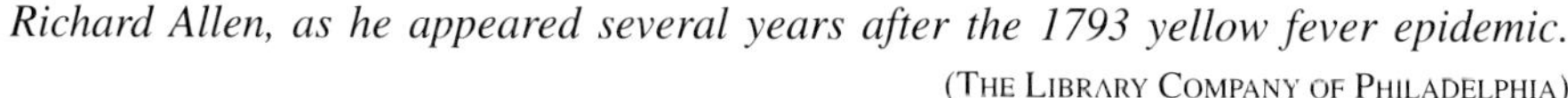

Richard Allen, as he appeared several years after the 1793 yellow fever epidemic.
(THE LIBRARY COMPANY OF PHILADELPHIA)

being done by Philadelphia's blacks. "I dont know what the people would do," he said in his letter to his brother, "if it was not for the Negroes, as they are the Principal nurses."

This battalion of heroes ventured out into the stricken city every day without fail. "Thus were many of the nurses circumstanced," Jones and Allen would note, "alone, until the patient died, then called away to another scene of distress, and thus have been a week or ten days left to do the best they could without sufficient rest, many of them having some of their dearest connexions sick at the time and suffering for want while their husband, wife, father, mother have been engaged in the service of the white people."

As the days wore on, they took more and more of the burden of caring for the city's ill. When the men hauling victims to Bush Hill reported the appalling conditions there, the Free African Society sent nurses. With most carpenters gone from the city, the supply of coffins soon ran out. The society set about purchasing boards and constructing coffins.

And then the inevitable happened. Traveling through the diseased city, venturing into stifling alleyways, blacks began coming down with the fever. Suddenly, almost overnight, scores of them were seized with the same horrible symptoms as their white neighbors. Richard Allen fell ill, and Absalom Jones had to shoulder the entire burden of keeping the relief effort organized.

As more and more blacks sickened and then died, a shudder went though the white community. What would happen if blacks responded to the pestilence in the same way as whites, with panic and flight? Who would be left to deal with the sick and dead? "If the disorder should continue to spread among them," a very gloomy Benjamin Rush commented, "then will the measure of our suffering be full."

PHILADELPHIA,

13*th* SEPTEMBER, 1793.

THE FEDERAL GAZETTE.

Died laſt night, at his ſeat, in Benſalem, Bucks County, FRANCIS XAVIER DUPONT, Conſul of the French Republic, at Philadelphia. He was a firm Patriot, and an honeſt man.

WE have good authority, to aſſure the Public, that the recovery of the Secretary of the Treaſury, and his lady, is confirmed, and that a ſervant girl in the family, who attended Mrs. Hamilton, having been afflicted with the complaint, and having had the ſame treatment for it, is alſo in a fair way of recovery.—This is a ſtrong confirmation of the goodneſs of the plan, purſued by Doctor Stevens, and ought to recommend it to the ſerious conſideration of our Medical Gentlemen. In ſuch a caſe, the pride of theory, ought to give way to fact and experience.

Preventative againſt the raging Yellow Fever.

IT has been ſuggeſted, with much appoſiteneſs of reaſoning, by no means unworthy of attention, that, to avoid being infected with the epidemic malady now prevailing in this metropolis, it is neceſſary to breakfeſt early, and that without thoſe appendages of the tables commonly called *Reliſhes*, whether of fiſh or fleſh. To avoid laſſitud and fatigue, as much as may be; and to dine moderately, on freſh animal and vegetable food, about one o'clock in the day; drinking Beer, Cyder, or good Brandy, reſpectively diluted with water, as the wholeſomeſt beveridge at meals. In the evening, Tea or Coffee may be drank, with ſimple Bread and Butter, as in the morning; but ſuppers are to be avoided. Dram drinking, (which ſome perſons practiſe in the morning, and indeed at other times of the day,) is at all times an evil and deſtructive habit; but at *preſent*, is doubly pernicious in its effects.

der at preſent raging at Philadelphia—by giving it a place in your paper, you may oblige a number of your readers.

Preventative.

Take 1 oz. of Salts, 1-2 in the evening, and 1-2 in the morning, mixt with manna; abſtain from the uſe of ſpiritous liquors and ſalt meat, and drink but moderately of Wine. Let your conſtant drink be lemonade, or water mixt with molaſſes; mix an equal proportion of nitre and camphor, make the ſame into pills, and take two or three daily.

The Cure.

In the firſt ſtage, or at all times, adminiſter a gliſter of warm warter, one quarter vinegar, to be repeated about every three or four hours, or oftener if neceſſary; drink copiouſly of lemonade, mixt with a litle nitre—if the patient ſhould be advvnced in the diſeaſe, take one of the pills mentioned in the preventative, every two hours.

New York, September 11.

Arrived—Ship Active, Seaman Liverpool; Brig Eliza, Elkins Havre-de-Grace; Dædalus, Stanley Cadiz.

The ſhip Favorite, Capt. Storey arrived at Cadiz all well.

The Ship Hibernian, Capt. Maſh arrived at Cadiz all well.

Captain Stanley, of the brig Dædalus, arrived here yeſterday from Cadiz. Spoke on the 25th Auguſt, in lat. 36, long. 56½, the ſnow———, Captain Perry, from Rhode Iſland, bound to the coaſt of Guinea, out 12 days, all well.

AT a meeting of a number of citizens, held at the court-houſe this evening, in conſequence of a verbal appointment of the Mayor and others convened at the city-hall, to take into conſideration the preſent calamitous ſtate of the city and its environs, having, in company with the overſeers of the poor, made inquiry into the ſituation of the poor and afflicted, are of the opinion, that, as it is not in the power of the overſeers to afford the neceſſary aid that the caſes of the ſick require, that the citizens be again convened, that Some effectual means may be adopted, to mitigate and, if poſſible, to afford relief to the afflicted.

Dr. R
further,
attendin
preſent,
ing the
tion wil
the ſick
of the af
attendan
While
mortal,
ing it,
Ruſh adv
City. At
vice to be
the diſea
medicine
now wiſh
not avoi
them. T
medical a
fection i
their bo
former di
Dr. R.
prudent f
the count
ter *froſt*, o
both of w
the conta
Sept. 1

To THE
COL.
O

Gentl

AS th
College h
ticable, I
communic
ther obſer
epidemic.
I have
not only i
full and q
and *tenſe*.
where the
a minute,
it. The
more freq
the pulſe
ed ſtate of
in a preter
pils of the

CHAPTER SIX

The Prince of Bleeders

In this awful situation, the stoutest hearts began to fail. Hope flickered, and despair succeeded distress in almost every countenance.

—Dr. Benjamin Rush, 1805

Thursday, September 12. Benjamin Rush found himself exhausted and near collapse as the day drew to a close. It wasn't simply that since the College of Physicians had met he had spent every waking minute seeing patients, usually over one hundred a day. Rush had yellow fever.

"My body became highly impregnated with the contagion. My eyes were yellow, and sometimes a yellowness was perceptible in my face," he noted. His sleep was irregular, and he frequently woke to find his bed linens soaked through with his own sweat. "These sweats were so offensive," he wrote, "as to oblige me to draw the bed-clothes close to my neck, to defend myself from their smell."

Despite the aches, despite dizziness and nausea, despite it all, Rush still saw and advised patients. He had to. He believed that he was one of the few physicians still seeing the nearly 6,000 persons then ill with the fever. So he struggled on, day after exhausting day. "When it was

Opposite: *From* The Federal Gazette, *September 13, 1793.*
(The Library Company of Philadelphia)

Benjamin Rush was arguably the most famous and respected doctor in the United States when the yellow fever epidemic began. (THE LIBRARY COMPANY OF PHILADELPHIA)

evening I wished for morning; and when it was morning, the prospect of the labours of the day . . . caused me to wish for the return of evening."

Word of Rush's illness spread and increased the citizens' fear. A number of well-known doctors had abandoned their patients and scampered to safer air; ten others had died, while still more were ill and could not receive patients. But from the moment the fever first began to claim victims, Dr. Rush had been a tower of energy and care, an ever-present Good Samaritan.

Now that he was ill, what would happen to the people who relied on him? More alarming still, Rush had recently announced that he had an absolute cure for the disease, something no other doctor had claimed. If Rush died—if his cure failed to save him—then all hope would vanish and the fever would march on unobstructed.

Rush did not happen upon his cure easily or immediately. During the earliest days of the fever Rush had treated patients with great caution. Doctors of that era believed in what was called *vis medicatrix naturae,* the healing power of nature. In other words, the body took its own measures to rid the humors of poisons and set them in balance once again; the doctor's job was to coax the body along in this process.

For the most part, medical treatment was very gentle. Herb teas were prescribed to break a slight fever. A glass of brandy would help a restless patient get to sleep.

Of course, some symptoms required slightly more drastic measures to effect a cure. If a doctor suspected a patient's intestines were blocked, he might use a few drops of a poisonous substance to induce vomiting and diarrhea. Bloodletting, or phlebotomy, was also practiced. In this procedure, a vein was opened and a small amount of blood was drawn off into a bowl. With a tad less blood, the theory went, the remaining blood would flow more freely and normally through the body.

Bloodletting was an ancient and trusted medical practice that had been in use for more than 2,500 years. Patients were bled to relieve headaches, depression, disease, and anxiety. Even a broken bone would bring out the lance and bowl. The various symptoms of yellow fever also called for bloodletting.

At the beginning of the epidemic, Rush used mild purges and moderate bleedings and urged patients to sit in cool air, take cold baths, and eat light meals. This clearly wasn't enough, because his patients continued to die.

After he visited with Mrs. LeMaigre and determined that she was battling yellow fever, Rush began to change his tactics. If the patient failed to show immediate improvement with mild treatments, he stepped up his attack. He administered bark (the shaved root of a tree such as dogwood) along with wine, brandy, and aromatics, such as ginger or cinnamon. He tried to sweat the fever out of a patient by coating various parts of his or her body with a thick salve composed of herbs and chemicals. These applications were called blisters, because they often irritated the skin enough to turn it a livid red. "Finding them all ineffectual, I attempted to rouse the system by wrapping the whole body . . . in blankets dipped in warm vinegar."

Nothing worked, and more and more of Rush's patients went to the grave. Each death shook him personally. In a letter to his Julia, Rush's anguish is clear: "You can recollect how much the loss of a single

---

Benjamin Rush received hundreds of frantic notes begging his help, such as this one written by Revolutionary War hero Thaddeus Kosciusko during the 1797 yellow fever epidemic. (THE HOUGHTON LIBRARY/HARVARD UNIVERSITY)

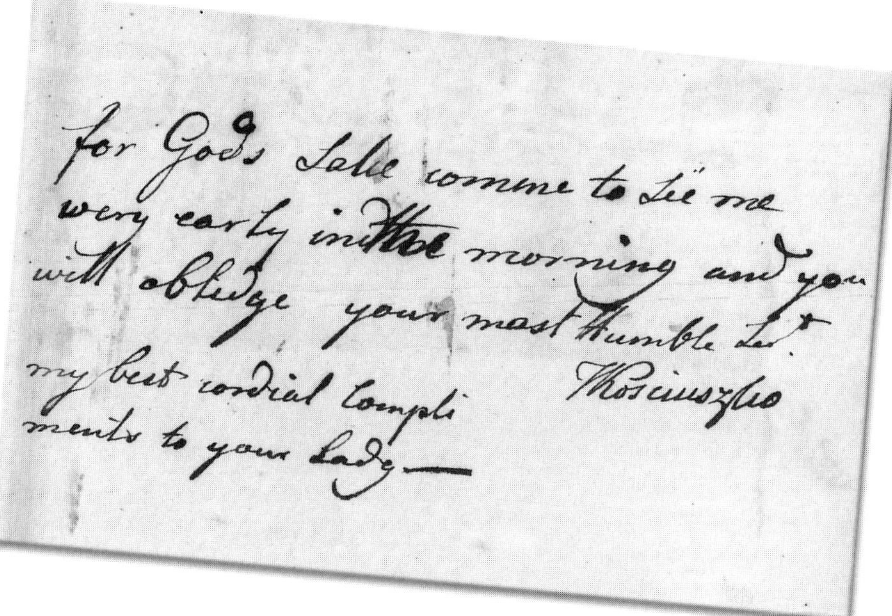

for God's Sake comme to See me
wery early inthe morning and you
will obliedge your most Humble Ser.t
my best cordial Compli- T Kosciuszko
ments to your Lady—

patient in a month used to affect me. Judge then how I must feel, in hearing every morning of the death of three or four!"

Another doctor might have thrown up his hands in bewilderment and admitted defeat. Not Benjamin Rush. He believed firmly that every illness had a cure and that all he had to do to discover it was to work harder. He spent every minute he could rummaging through his library, searching for some bit of information that might show him the light. It was while poring over his old medical books that he came upon John Mitchell's letter about the yellow fever plagues that had occurred in Virginia some fifty years before.

One of Mitchell's observations leaped off the page for Rush. Mitchell asserted that as soon as the stomach and intestines filled with blood, they had to be emptied at all costs. Otherwise, the blood would turn putrid and stop the body from its normal process of healing.

Mitchell also advised physicians to put aside any "ill-timed scrupulousness about the weakness of the body" and purge the patient ruthlessly. Instead of merely helping nature to heal the body, Mitchell was telling doctors to command and direct it along the proper course.

Rush then decided to try the strongest purge he knew of, known as the "Ten-and-Ten." Last used during the Revolutionary War, this recipe called for the patient to swallow ten grains (not quite one-third of an ounce) of calomel (mercury) and ten grains of jalap (the poisonous root of a Mexican plant related to the morning glory that was dried and powdered before ingesting). Both were highly toxic, and the body would work hard to expel them. Rush would, in effect, poison a patient in order to produce extreme vomiting and diarrhea.

His first use of this treatment seemed to work, even though he had to force the concoction down his patient's throat. He then decided to speed up the process by increasing the dosage to ten and fifteen and administering it three times in a single day, until it resulted in five large evacuations.

Rush next began experimenting with the amount of blood he would remove from the body in an effort to reduce inflammation. He, like most doctors then, believed that the human body held approximately twenty-five pounds of blood. Since the body actually holds less than half of this amount, most people who were bled so drastically passed out at some point in the procedure. For Rush, and for other doctors as well, this was simply a sign that the treatment was indeed working.

Few doctors kept accurate records on recovery rates during the yellow fever plague. But since Rush saw improvement in those he treated, he sensed that his cure was working, and working well. On September 3 he claimed that eight out of twelve patients had gotten better with just one treatment. The next day saw nine out of ten over the fever. By September 5 he was able to write Julia that "I now save 29 out of 30 of all to whom I am called on the first day [of their illness]."

Many doctors disputed Rush's cure rate and felt his "Ten-and-Fifteen" purge and copious bleedings dangerous. Dr. Adam Kuhn called the mercury and jalap drink "a murderous dose" and said so in the newspapers. Dr. Jean Devèze, a recent French arrival, condemned Rush with a passion: "He, I say, is a scourge more fatal to the human kind than the plague itself would be."

Other doctors agreed with Kuhn and Devèze and put forward their own treatments, though no one claimed to have found an absolute cure, as Rush did. Almost every one of them called for much milder methods than Rush's. Dr. William Currie completely rejected Rush's bloodletting and the use of mercury, saying such methods "cannot fail of being certain death." Instead, he suggested modest purging, that patients be gently induced to sweat, that their hands and feet be bathed in vinegar and water, and that they get as much cool, fresh air as possible.

Rush took any challenge, whether from a disease or from a colleague, as a personal attack to be confronted and conquered. When his ideas were questioned, he sensed a malicious conspiracy and counterattacked: "Besides combatting with the yellow fever, I have been obliged to contend with the prejudices, fears and falsehoods of several of my brethren, all of which retard the progress of truth and daily cost our city many lives."

Those he challenged fired back with equal ferocity. Ebenezer Hazard refused Rush's treatment as extreme, saying, "He . . . would order blood enough . . . drawn to fill [a] helmet, with as little ceremony as a mosquito would fill himself upon your leg."

This wasn't a behind-closed-doors disagreement, either. It was carried on in the city's newspapers, so that all citizens knew of the dispute. Some even joined in with their own opinions. From his upstate New York retreat where he and his wife were recuperating, Secretary of the Treasury Alexander Hamilton wrote to praise the cure used by his doctor, who had openly rejected Rush's cure. The secretary of war, Henry Knox, also followed the public feuding, and wrote: "The different opinions of the treatment excite great inquietude—But Rush bears down all before him."

Then Rush fell ill, and everyone waited to see what would happen.

To his credit, Rush did not hesitate to use his own cure. He turned himself over to two of his young assistants, who bled him and administered the purge. It would be months before Rush truly regained his strength, but within five days he was back on his feet and valiantly seeing patients in his home. On September19 he hired a horse-drawn carriage and began visiting patients again.

His fever lingered on, his cough worsened, and climbing stairs was difficult, but in Rush's mind his treatment had produced yet another cure. "Thus you see," he wrote to Julia, "that I have proved upon my own body that the yellow fever when treated in the new way, is no more than a common cold."

People now flocked to his home for the cure. One hundred fifty a day sought him out; his five assistants each saw thirty patients a day. They bled so many and so aggressively that they ran out of vessels to hold the blood. In the end they were forced to perform this procedure out-of-doors, bleeding patients directly onto the paving stones of the road.

Neither Rush nor his assistants could handle the press of sick people demanding his cure. Rush then showed members of the Free African

Barbers often substituted for doctors prior to the nineteenth century. This lithograph depicts an unhappy patient having blood drawn by a local barber while a curious bystander peers over his shoulder. (THE COLLEGE OF PHYSICIANS OF PHILADELPHIA)

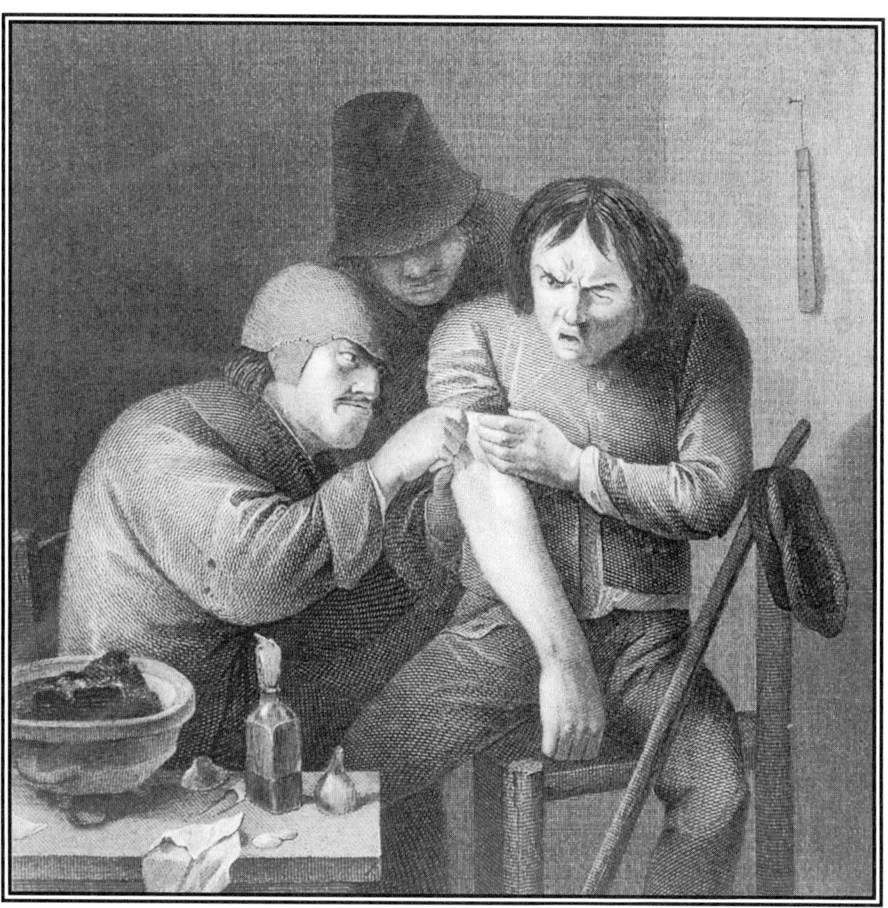

Society how to drain blood from a patient and they marched out to perform over 800 bleedings. Even Rush's eleven-year-old servant boy, Peter, was trained to open a vein and sent out to see the sick.

In reality, Rush's cure probably did more harm than good. Yet he never lost faith in it, never doubted it. Not even when three of his assistants and his beloved sister, Rebecca, died did he doubt. Why should he? Every day he received letters thanking him for his cure; every day hundreds of desperate people lined up outside his door or sent him frantic notes asking for his help.

While a handful of his colleagues embraced his cure, most of Philadelphia's doctors condemned his methods and dubbed Rush the "Prince of Bleeders." Yet they may have judged him too harshly. Medicine was in a curious state of transition at the end of the eighteenth century—groping toward more scientific and precise explanations of diseases, while still clinging to beliefs hundreds and even thousands of years old that were rooted in mythology and folk tales. Rush's treatment was based on accepted (if extreme) medical principles of the time and tested under the pressure of a raging plague. Maybe even more important, it gave the average citizen—trapped in Philadelphia and at the mercy of the mysterious killer—cause for hope. Dr. Benjamin Rush was, after all, living proof that the disease could be beaten.

Rush became a hero, and his fame soon spread beyond Philadelphia. Circuit Judge William Bradford, after hearing a number of stories about Rush's bravery and cures, wrote, "He is become the darling of the common people & his humane fortitude & exertions will render him deservedly dear."

So formidable was his reputation that Benjamin Rush could stride into a sickroom and calmly tell a suffering individual: "You have nothing but the yellow fever."

fail in four days. For freight or
pply to the master on board, at
's wharf, or to
WM. ROBINSON, jun.
No. 153, South Front-street.
d4t

Port-au-Prince,
The BRIG
LYDIA,
SAMUEL RINKER, Master,
il the 15th instant; has good ac-
ions for passengers—For passage
y to Messrs.
DUTILH and WACHSMUTH.
Oct. 7. dtf

le Port-au-Prince,
Le BRIG
LYDIA,
Capitaine SAMUEL RINKER,
RA pour le dit lieu le 15 courant.
voudront patter, voudront bien
a
DUTILH and WACHSMUTH.
hie, le 7 8bre, 1793. dtf

Edenton, (N. C.)
The SCHOONER
JOLLY TAR,
JOHN GALLOP, Master.
n Thursday next. For freight
pply to the master on board at
arf, or to
Wm. CLARK,
Near the Drawbridge.

OR BOSTON,
The Schooner
MARIA,
JOHN HILLS, Master,
g at Landenberger's dock. For
ssage, apply to the Captain on
Oct. 5. d4t

rt de Paix and
Le Borgne,
with all convenient speed.
The American BRIG
HANNAH,
Capt. DAVIDSON,
or passage, apply to
ouis Osmont,
No. 40, North Third-street.
dtf

Alexandria,
(In Virginia)
The new Sloop
HARMONY,
S DENICK, Master,
at Elliston and John Prat's
will take in freight on Friday
the next week. For freight
rd, or to JOSEPH BUR
r the Old Ferry.
d 10t

rives here in three days. List of each day's
drawing to be seen by those who wish to purchase.

J. HOPE.

Sept. 30th, 1793. dtf

A CARGO OF BEST
LISBON SALT,
Now delivering at Stamper's Wharf below
the Bridge, to be sold by
Levi Hollingsworth.
4th Oct. 1793. d7t.

DOCTOR RUSH'S
Celebrated Mercurial Purging & Sweating
POWDERS,
For preventing and curing the Prevailing
Putrid Fever, may be had, carefully prepa-
red, with proper directions, at
BETTON & HARRISON's,
No. 10, South Second-street.
Sept. 14. dtf.

All Persons indebted to
the Estate of John Strawbridge, of the city
of Philadelphia, deceased, are requested to
make immediate payment; and those having any demands, against the same, are desired to bring their accounts properly authen-
ticated that they may be paid, by
JAMES STRAWBRIDGE,
Acting Executor.
Sept. 24, 1793. dtf.

All persons indebted to
The estate of Samuel Merian, of the city
of Philadelphia, deceased, are requested to
make payment without delay, and those having any demands against said estate are requested to produce them duly proved to the
subscriber. PETER LEMAIGRE,
Sept. 30. dtf. Administrator.

All persons indebted to
The estate of John Townes, of the city of
Philadelphia, deceased, are requested to
make payment without delay, and those having any demands against said estate, are requested to produce them duly proved to the
subscriber. PETER LEMAIGRE,
Sept. 30. dtf, Administrator.

All persons indebted to
the estate of JOHN DUNKIN, late of the city
of Philadelphia, merchant, deceased, are requested to make immediate payment; and
those having any demands against the same,
are desired to bring them in (that they may
be settled) to either of the subscribers.
ANN DUNKIN, Administratrix.
ROBERT HENRY DUNKIN,
JOHN BARCLAY, Administrators.
Aug. 30. d 1m

Wheat for Sale.
3000 BUSHELS
VIRGINIA WHEAT,
Of excellent quality, now stored in the city.
For terms apply to Mr. A. SERVICE, No.
73, South Front-street, or the subscriber, at
his present residence.
EMANUEL WALKER.
Chesnut-Hill, 5th Oct. 1793. d6t

For Freight or Charter,
To any port in the W. In-
dies or the United States,
The Schooner
BETSEY,
BURTHEN 800 bbls. now lying at Wilmington, and ready to take in a cargo. For
terms apply to REED and FORDE,
at No. 51, South Front-street,
or at Wilmington.
Philad. Oct. 7. m w&s 10t

THE SCHOONER
JAMES,
Now lying a little below the
Drawbridge, a stout well built vessel, an A-
merican bottom, will carry about 400 bar-
rels flour.
To be Sold,
with all her materials as she came from
sea. Apply at No. 16 South Front Street, to
EVANS & HUNT.
Philad. Sept. 20 mw&f 1m

To be Sold,
For four or five years, as may be agreed upon, the owner intending to liberate her
after that period,
A MULATTO GIRL,
ABOUT 24 years of age, an excellent servant, and can be well recommended for her
honesty, sobriety and capacity. Enquire at
the office of the Federal Gazette.
Oct. 7. mw&f tf

One Guinea Reward.
RUN away a few days since, a French
Negro Man, of the Congo nation, named JACQUE; he is about 22 years of age,
is 5 feet & 1-2 inches high; has the name
Parasau, imprinted on his left breast.—When
he absconded, he had on a white shirt, long
trowsers, and a woolen jacket; carrying his
blanket, &c. rolled up, behind him.—Whoever brings the said run away slave to Mr.
Francis's Hotel, in fourth street, shall receive the above reward, besides all reasonable
expences, paid by
MADAME PESERRES.
Sept. 23. mw & f3t.

STILLS.
AN ASSORTMENT
WARRANTED STILLS,
FROM 20 to 200 gallons, for Sale at No.
74, South Water and No. 75 South
Front Street, on reasonable terms. Where
orders for any article in the Copper Smith's
line, will be observed with punctuality and
thanks by
Robert Orr.
July 20. ws&f.

Just Arrived,
AND FOR SALE,
By SAMUEL CLARKSON.
Old London Particular, Ditto. London, } Madeira Wine in Pipes, Hhds. & quarter Casks.
Sept. 12 w&s2m.

...fuch ...
be chear...
time agr...
a second...
family's...
suggest a...
easily eff...
ly, and ...
would in...
yourselve...
house in...
days, wh...
regulatio...
down a...
chearfull...
carriages...
accommo...
place, pl...
shall chea...
do leave ...
You...
th...

Signe...

Euro...
Received...

L...
No in...
think it p...
found its...
designs of...
mies. T...
with grea...
much har...
vide their...
of uncerta...
at present...
July there...
the neigh...
the Frenc...
the conqu...
upon the...
movement...
appears th...
sions are f...
of French...
of conside...
be remem...
last campa...
under Ge...
der in chie...
position to...
In the ...
have gaine...
stores of a...
Valencien...
Lille ha...
ed, and it...
that the bl...
ed compl...
liere) wh...
that town,...
accused of...
the garriso...
But among...
the remai...
which is ...
probability...
Dunkirk,...

CHAPTER SEVEN

"By Twelve Only"

Ye unfeeling savages! Ye monsters in the shape of men! Remember that your judge will probably, one day, say to you, "I was a stranger and ye took me not in, depart from me ye workers of iniquity."

—"A. B." IN *THE FEDERAL GAZETTE*, OCTOBER 1793

Saturday, September 14. As Mayor Clarkson approached city hall that morning, he carried with him the full weight of his city's almost complete collapse. He knew, for instance, that the courts had all but ceased to operate, committees were not meeting, the work of the Guardians had come to a stop, and Bush Hill was in turmoil despite the heartfelt efforts of the black volunteers there.

One after another, the city's newspapers had suspended operations, until only Andrew Brown's *Federal Gazette and Philadelphia Daily Advertiser* was being published daily; the *National Gazette,* under the editorial direction of Philip Freneau, appeared from time to time. Taverns were closing for lack of customers, and the street markets remained deserted. Doctors were openly disputing every aspect of the fever, and the College of Physicians, which had promised to meet every Monday, had given up. Even the blacks of the Free African Society—

OPPOSITE: *From* The Federal Gazette, *October 9, 1793.*
(THE LIBRARY COMPANY OF PHILADELPHIA)

the only ones actually doing anything in an organized, citywide way—were coming down with the disease.

That is why the mayor and a small group of citizens had taken the drastic and illegal step of calling for the formation of a special committee to run Philadelphia. Clarkson and his committee had, in effect, seized control of the government. If he needed proof that this was a necessary action, it greeted him that morning at the steps of city hall. There Clarkson had to push his way through a crowd of vendors selling coffins and patent medicine cures.

Aside from the mayor, the committee was made up of twenty-six individuals, though illness and death soon reduced their numbers. In the end, the business of running all of Philadelphia was, as Clarkson would write, "principally conducted by twelve only."

One of the first decisions made by the committee was to borrow $1,500 for the purchase of medicine, coffins, and a variety of other necessary items, as well as to pay for doctors, nurses, and gravediggers. All told, the committee would spend $37,647.19 to combat the sickness that infested their city. This is a great deal of money even today, but in 1793 it was a fortune. What is more, the members of the committee could be held personally responsible for all of this money because they had no legal authority to borrow or spend it.

The magnitude of this responsibility and the courage of the committee members become clear when we learn that the majority of them were not wealthy. They were, as the mayor himself put it, "mostly taken from the middle walks of life." One of them was an umbrella maker; another built cabinets; another, chairs. Two carpenters volunteered, as did a teacher, a mechanic, a coach builder, and a playing-card maker. If they were compelled to repay even a portion of the debt, it would ruin most of them financially. Yet they overcame their fears and took on the responsibility in order to save their stricken city and its people.

As president of the committee, Clarkson presided over its daily meeting and helped organize its operation. Specific assignments were then handed out to members. Henry Deforest took on the formidable task of providing food for the city; Samuel Benge took charge of carrying the sick to Bush Hill and seeing that the dead were properly buried.

Once the committee began to act, it was everywhere. The members went street by street to catalogue the number of houses boarded up, infected, and open. The homes of dead fever victims were cleaned to remove the "seeds of its infection." Because relatives were sometimes impossible to locate, the committee began to administer the estates of the deceased who had no legal heirs or executors available. After the potter's field and Bush Hill cemeteries were full, they took over the public square nearest Bush Hill and began burying paupers there.

Out of a committee of supremely enterprising and resourceful members, one managed to outshine the rest in the range of activities he assumed. His name was Israel Israel, a reserved, forty-seven-year-old tavern keeper and merchant. When the first orphans were found huddled near a blacksmith's forge, Israel and two others were given the task of finding shelter, care, and support for them. A house was rented, a matron hired, and provisions carted to the door of this new city institution. As more and more children turned up, the Orphan Committee's burden increased in scope until it was caring for 192 children.

But Israel's work did not end with helping Philadelphia's orphans. When complaints came in about the foul smells wafting from the potter's field—smells that many feared were spreading the disease—Israel went with James Sharswood to personally inspect burial procedures. It was Israel who was asked to arrange for the harvesting of grain at Bush Hill; and it was Israel again who headed the Committee of Distribution, the group responsible for warehousing and handing out food, firewood, and clothes to the city's growing number of needy families.

Israel's patience, strength, and ingenuity were tested every day of the plague. It was Israel who went to the almshouse to persuade that

Israel Israel was a wealthy man who dedicated much of his spare time to helping less fortunate Philadelphians. (The Abby Aldrich Rockefeller Folk Art Museum, Colonial Williamsburg Foundation, Williamsburg, Va.)

institution to open its doors to additional paupers, Israel who met with the angry owner of Bush Hill the minute he returned to town to work out fair compensation. He had been called on to help, and he helped in every way possible.

Soon after being established, the original committee divided itself up into a variety of subcommittees. Each subcommittee handled a specific duty, such as obtaining five hundred cords of wood before winter set in, cleaning the streets, or distributing cash to those in need.

By far the most desperate situation was at Bush Hill. Medical student Charles Caldwell helped out for a few days and then left. The four doctors appointed to attend the patients rarely showed up. Two of them made a number of visits but spent more time performing autopsies on dead bodies than ministering to the sick. When the Guardians ceased performing their duties, it meant there was no one to supervise the place at all.

The black nurses did their best to care for, comfort, and clean up the sick and dying, but their task was overwhelming. In September the average number of deaths per day began to rise at an alarming rate, and relatives and neighbors hurried anyone they suspected of having yellow fever off to Bush Hill. "Poor people," Mathew Carey noted, "[were] forced . . . to that hospital, though labouring under only common colds and common fall fevers."

Over one hundred people now jammed the mansion, and the dead lay unburied. As a member of the mayor's committee, Mathew Carey had a special understanding of conditions at Bush Hill. "The sick, the dying, and the dead were indiscriminately mingled together," he recalled. "The ordure and other evacuations of the sick, were allowed to remain in the most offensive state imaginable. . . . It was, in fact, a great human slaughter-house."

The committee sent a delegation to the house, and a list of needed items was drawn up and ordered. A carpenter was found to build beds; a horse, cart, and attendants were hired to bring in the sick and carry out the dead. And then two committee members, Peter Helm, a barrel maker, and Stephen Girard, a wealthy merchant, did an amazing thing: They volunteered to personally manage Bush Hill.

We don't know much about Peter Helm. He was skilled enough at his woodworking that the ever-demanding President Washington employed him several times to make objects for his household. He was also a devout member of the Moravian congregation, a Christian denomination that accepted the Bible as the sole source of faith and practice. When Helm read Psalm 9:18, "For the needy shall not always be forgotten; the expectation of the poor shall not perish for ever," he knew his duty was to serve them. When he read a little later, in Psalm

23:4, "Yea, though I walk through the valley of the shadow of death, I will fear no evil," he knew he would be safe.

Helm was a humble man who brought to Bush Hill three enduring qualities—an established work ethic, an endless supply of kindness, and an indomitable spiritual courage.

Much more is known about the forty-three-year-old Stephen Girard. He was French-born, blind in one eye, and he detested inefficiency and failure. As one of Philadelphia's wealthiest citizens, he could have fled the city, as others from his economic class had done. But he didn't. He had business to attend to, and besides, he did not believe the illness ravaging his city was a contagious plague. He held to this opinion even though he contracted a mild case of yellow fever during the last week of August, the sort of near miss that frightened many other citizens into either hiding indoors or fleeing to the countryside.

Girard brought along a calm personality, a steely determination, and an unerring sense of organization.

And so Peter Helm and Stephen Girard marched off to Bush Hill in mid-September. Noting his assignment in his private papers, Girard added, "I shall accordingly be very busy for a few days." In fact, Helm and Girard would faithfully attend to what came to be known as the pest house for sixty straight days.

The first thing they did at Bush Hill was to divide the chores. Helm dealt with what went on outside the building, while Girard directed what happened within.

Helm established a simple system for receiving new patients and having the dead carted away for burial. He set up an area where coffins could be made, provided decent housing for the nurses and other staff members, had the barn converted so those recovering from their illness could be kept apart from the newly ill, and found storage for supplies. He even had the pumps repaired so that fresh water could be provided to patients for the first time.

Girard's task was even more daunting. First, the interior of the mansion had to be cleaned from top to bottom. Patients were then put in separate rooms, with the dying in one, the "very low" in another, and so on. Every room and hallway had at least one assigned nurse, most of whom were volunteers from the Free African Society; and because delirious patients sometimes wandered off, a doorkeeper was stationed at the entrance to keep track of who came and went.

Setting up such an organized hospital was hard enough; keeping it operating was even more difficult. As a hot, humid September limped along, the death rate in the city leaped to over sixty a day, and more and more wretchedly ill people were shipped off to Bush Hill, often in the final stages of sickness. The number of patients rose as the fever raged on, with as many as 140 crammed into the mansion.

Blind in his right eye, Stephen Girard still took on the formidable task of administering what went on inside the Bush Hill hospital. (THE COLLEGE OF PHYSICIANS OF PHILADELPHIA)

To handle the increase in patients, the committee ordered that a new structure be built to accommodate them. In the space of four days, a house sixty feet long and eighteen feet wide was erected, complete with two chimneys. Another structure was quickly assembled to store empty coffins and serve as a morgue.

The strain and pressure of operating Bush Hill might have driven less dedicated individuals to give up or ask for replacements. Helm and Girard stayed at their posts. Girard even helped care for patients. One anonymous witness was astonished by Girard's dedication and compassion, noting, "I even saw one of the diseased . . . [discharge] the contents of his stomach upon [him]. What did Girard then do? . . . He wiped the patient's cloaths, comforted [him] . . . arranged the bed, [and] inspired with courage, by renewing in him the hope that he should recover. —From him he went to another, that vomited offensive matter that would have disheartened any other than this wonderful man."

In a matter of days Bush Hill was put into decent operating order, and the spirits of the patients began to improve. But both Helm and Girard knew that one more element was needed if the hospital was to succeed: a full-time physician.

Once again, a dedicated individual came to the rescue. On September 16 a thirty-nine-year-old doctor and recent arrival to the city volunteered. His name was Jean Devèze.

It's very likely that Girard had a hand in getting Dr. Devèze to volunteer just when he needed him. Like Girard, Dr. Devèze was French; like Girard, he did not believe the fever was contagious; and like Girard, he did not believe in the Rush cure. Girard had condemned the extreme bleeding and purging as a "pernicious treatment" that "sent many of our citizens to another world."

At first there was some hesitation in the committee over hiring a French doctor. It would seem like a slap at all American doctors, and especially at Dr. Rush. The American doctors who had already failed the Bush Hill patients were so upset that they even promised to show up more regularly. The situation required several days of wrangling and discussions, but in the end Girard and Dr. Devèze won out.

Dr. Devèze had not only seen and treated yellow fever while living in the West Indies, he had contracted it twice. His treatment was cautious and gentle. Small amounts of sweetened wine would be given to a patient to stimulate the blood; quinine would be administered. For nourishment patients were given "veal or chicken broth, creamed rice, and tapioca." Some patients were bled, though only in very small amounts.

Let the body do its own healing, Dr. Devèze was saying. Clean up the patient and sickroom to remove noxious odors. Provide tea and broth and nontoxic medicine to help the body fight off the fever.

As conditions at the hospital improved, so did its reputation as a place of healing. When Helm and Girard took over, no one in the city wanted to be taken to Bush Hill, fearing it was a death sentence. By the end of September everything had changed. "No sooner was a Person affected with a headache," Dr. William Annan observed, "than he became anxious to be removed to Bushhill Hospital."

Despite growing evidence that the "French cure" was effective in keeping patients alive, it still came in for wide criticism. Benjamin Rush attacked the mild methods used by Jean Devèze and others, even though he had no real statistics to back his claims. "The French physicians are every where getting into disrepute," the increasingly combative Rush asserted. "They have . . . destroyed at least two thirds of all who have perished by the disorder."

Peter Helm, Stephen Girard, Dr. Devèze, and all the nurses and attendants did their best to ignore the controversy and labored on. And every day their fame grew. Later an anonymous author would issue *An Account of . . . the Malignant Fever.* In it, the writer detailed the amazing work and dedication that brought order and cleanliness to Bush Hill and included special praise for the two managers: "What rewards do these men deserve? who were instrumental in the lives of many! They gave up their own to help the helpless."

Bush Hill became a pocket of calm and hope, but it could not cure or comfort the entire population of Philadelphia. The city continued to stagger under the invisible invader's assault. As the days marched along, burials rose in number, reaching eighty on September 17. Elizabeth Drinker heard more stories of friends who had died, and lamented: "Desolution, Cruelty and Distress have of late resounded in our ears from many quarters." Even the ever-confident Dr. Rush mourned that "nothing but the power of the Almighty could stop it."

Inevitably, as Mathew Carey realized, the fear in Philadelphia began

---

As word of the epidemic spread, many towns near Philadelphia closed off communications with the city and placed guards at the entrances to their communities to keep out fever victims. (THE COLLEGE OF PHYSICIANS OF PHILADELPHIA)

At a MEETING of the INHABITANTS of the BOROUGH of
LANCASTER, held at LANCASTER, at the Courthouſe on Thurſday,
September 19th, 1793, to take into Conſideration the preſent alarm-
ing State of the MALIGNANT FEVER, which rages in the City of
Philadelphia.

RESOLVED, JASPER YEATES, in the Chair.

THAT we conceive it incumbent on ourſelves to adopt ſuch Reſolutions as may tend
to prevent the preſent MALIGNANT FEVER, which rages in the City of Philadelphia, and other Places, from ſpreading to this Borough.
Reſolved, THAT it be recommended to the Merchants and other Inhabitants, to refrain
from importing any Goods whatever into this Borough or the Vicinity thereof, during the
Period of four Weeks. (The Article of Salt from Places not infected, excepted.)
Reſolved, THAT we highly approve of the Recommendation of the Corporation
to the Proprietors of the Stages in this Place, to diſcontinue the running of the Stages
between the City of Philadelphia and this Borough, in Order to give Relief to the Minds
of the Inhabitants: And that we will uſe every Effort in our Power to prevent the run-
ning of the ſaid Stages and all other Carriages, during the Continuance of the preſent
EPIDEMICAL DISORDER, and to prevent diſeaſed and infectious Perſons from coming
into this Borough.
Reſolved, THAT eight Perſons he appointed in each Ward, to carry theſe Reſolves
into Execution, conjointly with the Wardens and Inſpectors of each Ward, two of the
Perſons ſo appointed to ſerve for one Week, and ſo in Rotation according to the following
Order:
For North-Eaſt Ward, Matthias Young, John Light, Samuel Boyd, Chriſtian Apple,
Samuel Humes, John Hambright, Chriſtian Petri, and Jacob Mayer.
North-Weſt Ward, Godlieb Nauman, William Reichenbach, Michael App, Abraham
Dehuff, Peter Bayer, Jacob Shæffer, Andrew Geiſs and Ludwig Heck.
South-Eaſt Ward, Jeremiah Moſhier, Adam Meſſencop, John Lightner, Leonard Eich-
holtz, Emanuel Reigart, John Franciſcus, Henry Pinkerton and Stophel Franciſcus.
South-Weſt Ward, John Bauſman, Jacob Graff, John Reitzel, Thomas Turner, Adam
Wilhelm, Chriſtopher Brunner, Jacob Bailey and Jacob Swartz.
And in Caſe of the ſaid Perſons ſhould decline to ſerve, the Corporation are requeſted
to appoint others in their Stead.
Reſolved, THAT it be recommended to the Corporation to engage Adam Hart and
Daniel Ehler to attend at the Bridge of Mr. Abraham Witmer, in Order to prevent an
Infraction of theſe Reſolves, and that the Sums for which they ſhall be ſo engaged, ſhall
be paid by a public Subſcription.
Reſolved, THAT the foregoing Reſolutions be publiſhed in Handbills.

JASPER YATES, Chairman.

to excite "the terror of the inhabitants of all neighboring states." In New Jersey the cities of Trenton and Lamberton resolved that "a total stop should be put to the landing of all persons from Philadelphia." The city of Winchester, Virginia, ordered "a guard at every avenue of the town leading from the Potomac, to stop all suspected persons, packages, etc., coming from Philadelphia."

Handbills like the one printed in Lancaster, Pennsylvania, were printed alerting citizens to "the present alarming State of the MALIGNANT FEVER, which rages in the City of Philadelphia." Armed patrols scouted country lanes and byways to prevent "diseased and infectious Persons from coming into this Borough."

Stagecoaches to and from Philadelphia were stopped; postmasters used tongs to dip mail and newspapers from the city in vinegar and other substances they thought would purify them. Emotions ran high, driven by fear of the unknown. In Milford, Delaware, a Philadelphia woman and her black servant were stopped on the road outside of town. Her wagon and all its contents were burned, and the woman was stripped, tarred and feathered, and, along with her servant, run off. Citizens in another Delaware town refused to allow one ship from Philadelphia to land and take on fresh water, and they attacked and sank another.

To be sure, some of these towns sent money and other items for Philadelphia's relief. Manhattan banned ships and travelers from the stricken town and posted guards at all arrival points, but its citizens also sent along $5,000 in aid. Other towns sent livestock, chickens, and carts of vegetables. From the Widow Grubb of Chester, New Jersey, came eighteen bundles of shirts and dresses for the orphans.

All donations were carefully recorded in a ledger by the committee and put to use. Still, this outpouring of charity could not change a new fact of life. Before the month of September was out, Philadelphians found themselves surrounded by scared and hostile neighbors. Even if they had wanted to flee, escape was now all but impossible.

LIST of the names of the perfons who died in Philadelphia, or in different parts of the union, after their departure from this city, from Auguft 1ft, to the middle of December, 1793*.

ABIGAIL, a negrefs
Jofeph Abbot
John Abel, fhoemaker
Henry Abel's child
John Abrahams, fhopkeeper
Elizabeth Abraham
James Ackley, labourer, wife, and three daughters,
John B. Ackley's child
Widow Ackley
James Adair, labourer, wife, and fon.
Hefter Adams
Mofes Adams, carpenter
Robert Adams's two children
Sarah Adams, fervant girl
Andrew Adgate, cardmaker
Widow Adgate and 2 children
Mary Addington
James Ager
Peter Agge, phyfician
Mary Advulter
John Ainey, ftone-cutter
John Alberger, cooper
Chriftian Alberger, fkinner
Jofeph Alberton, wife, and two children
Wife of Tho's Alberton, farmer
Frederic Albrecht
——— Albrecht, fkinner
Michael Albrecht's fon Michael
——— Antonio, clerk, Portugal
Andrew Apple, and child
Henry Apple, taylor
Elizabeth Appleby, fervant girl
Henry Apfel's daughter
Benjamin Armand and child
Chriftopher Arpurth's wife
Andrew Armftrong's child
Barney Armftrong, labourer
Chriftian Armftrong, weaver
Hugh Armftrong, weaver
Chriftopher Armftrong, weaver
James Armftrong, weaver
John Armftrong
Michael Artery
John Afh, breeches-maker
George Afhen
Nathaniel Afhby's child
John Afhton, labourer, and wife
Jofeph Afhton, bricklayer, wife, and two children
Jofeph Afhton, carpenter
Jofeph Afhtin
Stephen Afton, labourer
Kitty Auftin, feamftrefs
Peter Afton, merchant, wife, and fon
John Atkinfon
Caleb Attmore, hatter, and his apprentice
Jane Attrictz, wid. & daughter
James Aubaine
Phil. B. Audibert, merchant, Fr.
Monfieur Auje, Fr.
Julia Aulet, fervant girl
Ifaac Auftin, currier
Remiquis Azor
Prifcilla Alberton
James Alder, merchant
Thomas Allibone's child
Elifha Alexander, taylor
James Alexander, hatter
Jofeph Alexander, weaver, & apprentice
——— Alexander's wife, and an apprentice
Hefter Alexander
Rebecca Alexander
Nicholas Allaway, labourer
Auguftus Allbrink, & 3 children
Elizabeth Allegue
Ann Allen
James Allen's child

* This lift has been partly collected from the church-books of all the different congregations, and partly from the information received by feveral perfons who have been employed to make enquiry at every houfe in the city and liberties. Though very great pains have been taken, and expenfe incurred, in its arrangement, ftill it is not given as fully complete and accurate. But, it is hoped, that its defects and errors are but few, and, confidering the difficulty of the bufinefs, fuch only, as will meet the reader's ready indulgence.

CHAPTER EIGHT

"This Unmerciful Enemy"

Death, mounted on his pale horse, seemed to ride triumphant; there was but a step between the people in the city and the tomb.

—Elhanan Winchester, 1795

Saturday, October 12. The committee and its many subcommittees were in place and operating smoothly. Problems of every sort were being addressed and solved. Bush Hill had been turned around so thoroughly that people now clamored to be admitted. So many applied that patients had to have a doctor's certificate stating that they did indeed have yellow fever in order to be let in.

These efforts certainly had a calming effect on the populace, and the worst of the panic began to ease. But the fever showed no sign of relenting. If anything, it was gaining strength and deadliness. On Monday, October 7, a total of 82 dead were carted away for burial. Ninety died on Friday and 111 on Saturday. Tents were set up at the cemeteries so that gravediggers could rest but never be far from their ceaseless work.

The Reverend Mr. Helmuth was pondering "this unmerciful enemy" as he made his way through the city. Over the previous six days, 130 of

Opposite: *The first page of the list of the dead as it appeared in Mathew Carey's history of the epidemic, 1794.* (The Library Company of Philadelphia)

his Lutheran congregation had been carried off, and his church's tiny burial ground was looking more and more like a plowed field.

Could it be, he wondered, that Lutherans caught the sickness more readily than Quakers, Methodists, or Catholics? His Lutheran colleague the Reverend John Schmidt had the fever, and his parish gravedigger and the gravedigger's mother had already succumbed.

All this calamity surrounded Helmuth, but he stayed in the city and made daily door-to-door visits, cautiously walking deserted streets and abandoned alleyways "with a trembling heart." House after house was decorated with a tiny red flag, the sign that yellow fever had invaded it. Block after block was empty and still. Those few Philadelphians he encountered shunned him, just as they shunned the black nurses, gravediggers, carters of the dead, doctors, bloodletters, and anyone who worked at or even visited Bush Hill.

Nighttime was worse. Without the hired lamplighters, most of the city's 662 whale oil streetlamps remained unlit, the surrounding areas cast into a gloomy darkness. "Such a deep silence reigned in the streets [after nine o'clock]," Helmuth wrote. "I perfectly recollect several visits of the sick, which I had to make, entirely alone, at that time of the night. . . . Houses shut up to the right and left, deserted by their inhabitants, or containing persons struggling in death at that very time, or whose former inhabitants were all dead already."

Occasionally the stench of death would fill Helmuth's nose and demand his attention. On one block of narrow Appletree Alley he counted forty dead. Most often the minister was attracted by the pitiful shrieks and calls of the sick in the final stages of the disease.

Such distress upset and frightened him, but it also strengthened his conviction that Philadelphia had brought it all on itself. "After such a merry, sinful summer," he mused, "by the just judgement of God, a most mournful autumn followed."

The Reverend J. Henry C. Helmuth went through the stricken city to visit numerous stricken parishioners and later wrote an account of the plague.

(The Historical Society of Pennsylvania)

Helmuth wasn't the only one who realized that the fever was winning. On October 17 committee member Caleb Lownes wrote in the official minutes: "From the accounts received from different quarters of the city, it is evident that the disorder . . . has for the last week been more general and alarming than at any time since its appearance."

Even with his mercury-and-jalap cure in hand, Benjamin Rush looked about him and understood that Philadelphia itself might succumb at any moment. "Not a ray of alleviation of the present calamity breaks in our city from any quarter," he wrote to Julia. "All is a thick and melancholy gloom."

The weather did not help anyone's spirits. After rain fell on September 9, a warm, deadly dry spell followed, lasting over a month. "Many people . . . looked for rain," committee member John Bordley noted, "which they believed would be fatal to the infection. Others . . . looked only for mere cold, whether attended by rain or not, because histories of this fever assured them that cold had always been fatal to the infection."

Rain finally fell on October 12 and then again on October 15—a steady shower that Philadelphians hoped would clean the air of fatal odors and wash away the foul, disease-causing matter in the streets. Benjamin Rush felt the rain on his face and rejoiced: "The appearance of this rain was like a dove with an olive branch in its mouth."

Yet 111 died on October 12, and 103 the next day.

Clearly, the mysterious killing force was still in Philadelphia, still working its way into households despite every precaution, still infecting at an alarming rate. One man named Collins had lost his entire family—his wife, his two daughters, his son, and his son's wife and child—early in the plague. He married again and his new wife promptly died. Finally, at the height of the fever, his will to survive gave out. Mr. Collins caught the fever, and a few days later he joined the rest of his family members in the crowded potter's field.

More than just the fever was preying on those left in Philadelphia. The crime rate went up, and there was rioting. Few firsthand accounts make mention of the lawbreaking and violence. Apothecary shops were broken into and medicines stolen; food was taken from the few farmer's

During England's Black Plague of 1664, many of the dead were buried hastily in mass graves. Similar burials took place in Philadelphia in 1793.

(THE COLLEGE OF PHYSICIANS OF PHILADELPHIA)

wagons to appear in town. The committee decided to ignore the problem—at least on the public record—and concentrate instead on keeping people alive.

Benjamin Rush mentions the disruptions in a few brief references, but provides no details. The treasury clerk, Joshua Dawson, did note "fine doings in the River, easy means of smuggling, & most likely, little precaution taken to prevent it." Outsiders already looked upon Philadelphia as a blighted area. Why, these Philadelphia citizens probably decided, smudge the city's reputation even further—and possibly drive away future business—with detailed written accounts of looting and violence?

One thing they did mention was the grasping hand of the landlords. Tenants, made jobless by the fever, ran out of rent money and were turned out of their homes. Even famous and beloved citizens felt the landlord's bite. One day Benjamin Rush returned home to discover that his landlord (the annoyed owner of Bush Hill, William Hamilton) had raised his rent and was demanding three months' payment in advance.

The committee could not stop the evictions, but they did attempt to assist renters with small cash advances. These handouts were not meant to provide long-term assistance but rather to see the individual or family through the week ahead.

In a few instances the charity only lined the pockets of the greedy. One landlord told the committee that her tenants needed immediate financial help in order to survive and was granted the money requested. After pocketing the money herself, she seized her tenants' clothing and put everyone out on the street anyway. October seemed to have brought out the very worst in the fever and in many of Philadelphia's citizens.

It was during these terrible days that Benjamin Rush once again began to feel weak and feverish. Yellow fever had invaded his body for a second time. And despite his own insistence that his cure needed to be administered at the first signs of fever, he did not have himself bled or purged. He left no explanation for shunning his cure. Perhaps he felt his illness was mild in comparison to his first experience; perhaps one encounter with his cure was enough. Whatever the reason, Rush tried to ignore his condition and carried on his medical practice as best he could, visiting patients from morning to night.

His joints ached painfully. He had no appetite. And his terrible night sweats returned. When he did manage to nod off, his sleep was haunted by "disturbing and frightful dreams. The scenes of them were derived altogether from sick rooms and grave-yards." Still, he rose every morning and set off on his mission, often dressed in the same tattered and soiled clothes he had worn the day before.

He collapsed in a patient's room on October 4 and had to be carried home. He was up again two days later, but the yellow fever would not relent. He fainted again on October 9. Finally, he took his own cure once more.

"It puked me several times," he would record, "[and] next morning it operated downwards, and relieved me." This time, however, Rush did not rebound so quickly. He was confined to his bed, unable even to raise his head, for six straight days, during the absolute peak of the fever.

It did not seem that the situation could get much worse. Then reports began to filter in that the fever had appeared in the "out parts" of Philadelphia, what we would call the suburbs. Communities such as Frankford, Southwark, and the Northern Liberties trembled as cases appeared among them despite their efforts to keep it out. The plague seemed truly unstoppable.

There wasn't much anyone could do except carry on as best as pos-

MORTALITY.

—EACH MOMENT has its fickle, emulous
Of TIME's enormous scythe, whose ample sweep,
Strikes empires from the root; each MOMENT plays
His little weapon in the narrower sphere
Of sweet DOMESTIC comfort, and cuts down
The fairest bloom of sublunary bliss.

An Account of the BAPTISMS AND BURIALS in the United Churches of Christ Church and St. Peter's, by Matthew Whitehead and John Ormrod, Clerks; and Joseph Dolby, Sexton.

Also---An abstract of the Baptisms and Burials of the various Congregations of the City and Suburbs of Philadelphia. From December 25, 1792, to December 25, 1793.

BAPTISMS,	Males,	74	BURIALS, Males,	228
	Females,	65	Females,	170
		139		398

Difference of Baptisms and Burials in Christ Church and St. Peter's between this year and last,

Baptisms decreased	41	Burials increased,	373

Buried under one year,	23	From forty to fifty	37
From one to three	31	to sixty	31
to five	19	to seventy	19
to ten	26	to eighty	18
to twenty	42	to ninety	7
to thirty	81	to a hundred	1
to forty	63	to a hundred and five	1

The Diseases and Casualties in Christ Church and St. Peter's, this year.

Apoplexy,	1	Gravel	2
Asthma,	1	Hooping Cough	5
Bilious Fever	3	Hives	5
Cholic	1	Mortification	3
Cancer,	2	Nervous Fever	5
Child-bed,	3	Old Age	3
Consumption	12	Purging and Vomiting	9
Dry Gripes	1	Palsey	7
Dropsy	9	Small-pox	16
Decay	44	Suddenly	4
Fits	17	Teeth and Worms	10
Fever	7	Worms	6
Flux	6	Yellow Fever	214
Gout	2		

ST. PAUL's CHURCH.

Baptisms	143	Decreased	2	Burials	94	Increased	54

ROMAN CATHOLIC CHURCHES.

ST. MARY's	Baptisms	335	Decreased	13
	Burials	370	Increased	228
HOLY TRINITY,	Baptisms	53	Increased	6
	Burials	53	Increased	40

BAPTISMS INCREASED or DECREASED.

Swedes	42	Decreased	10
German Lutherans	506	Increased	66
Ditto Reformed	200	Decreased	1
First Presbyterians	45	Ditto	9
Second Do.	50	Ditto	26
Third Do.	60	Ditto	5
Scotch Do.			
The Associate Church	6	Decreased	2
Moravians	1	Ditto	6
Methodists	50	Ditto	30
Jews, or Hebrew Church	4		

(Printed by William W. Woodward, at Franklin's Head, No. 41, Chesnut-street)

BURIALS INCREASED or DECREASED.

Swedes	96	Increased	6[illegible]
German Lutherans	802	Ditto	617
Ditto Reformed	224	Ditto	151
The Friends	482	Ditto	343
First Presbyterians	95	Ditto	58
Second Do.	147	Ditto	86
Third Do.	152	Ditto	105
Scotch Do.	31	Ditto	23
The Associate Church	15	Ditto	9
Moravians	18	Ditto	10
Society of Free Quakers	43	Ditto	28
Methodists	50	Ditto	20
Baptists	87	Ditto	55
Jews, or Hebrew Church	4	Ditto	2

BURIALS in the STRANGER's GROUND.

Whites	1639	Increased	504
Blacks	305	Ditto	236

BAPTISMS this Year,	1634	Decreased	131
BURIALS Ditto,	5304	Increased	3939

BURIALS in the GRAVE-YARDS, since the FIRST of AUGUST.

Christ Church and St. Peter's	229	Roman Catholics—St. Mary's	278
St. Paul's	77	Ditto . . . Holy Trinity	30
Swedes	79	The Associate Church	18
German Lutherans	658	Moravians	15
Ditto Reformed	265	Society of Free Quakers	50
The Friends	385	Methodists	35
First Presbyterians	76	Baptists	72
Second Do.	129	Kensington,	178
Third Do.	112	Jews or Hebrew Church	4
Scotch Do.	18	Stranger's Ground	1426
		TOTAL since August	5019

HOW many precious souls are fled
To the vast regions of the dead!
Since to this day the changing sun
Through his last yearly period run.

We yet survive; but who can say?
That through this year, or month, or day,
"I shall retain this vital breath,
"Thus far, at least, in league with death."

That breath is thine, eternal God;
Tis thine to fix my soul's abode;
It holds its life from thee alone
On earth, or in the world unknown.

To thee our spirits we resign,
Make them and own them still as thine;
So shall they live secure from fear,
Though death should blast the rising year.

Thy children, panting to be gone,
May bid the tide of time roll on,
To land them on that happy shore,
Where years and death are known no more

No more fatigue, no more distress,
Nor sin, nor hell shall reach that place;
No groans to mingle with the songs,
Resounding from immortal tongues:

No more alarms from ghostly foes;
No cares to break the long repose;
No midnight shade, no clouded sun,
But sacred high eternal noon.

O, long expected year! begin:
Dawn on this world of woe and sin;
Fain would we leave this weary road,
To sleep in death, and rest with God.

The city government did not keep accurate records of yearly births and deaths and relied on information supplied by local churches. The number of deaths since August in this bill of mortality is given as just over 5,000, a very accurate estimate of the toll yellow fever took in 1793. (THE LIBRARY COMPANY OF PHILADELPHIA) sible. The committee continued to operate and solve problems; patients were cared for at Bush Hill; members of the Free African Society went door to door offering assistance; the few remaining doctors administered whatever medical attention they thought might work; and quacks offered a variety of home-brewed powders and teas.

Philip Freneau chose to combat the plague with denial and humor. As editor of the *National Gazette,* Freneau struggled as much to keep his paper in operation as he did to avoid the fever. Because supplies had become scarce after week two of the plague, Freneau had a hard time finding paper. Instead of the usual four to eight pages, he was often forced to publish a single sheet.

His *National Gazette* was also short on fever news. It avoided publishing most obituaries, never mentioned the rise in crime, and was vague about the spread of the disease. For real news, people turned to Andrew Brown's *Federal Gazette,* the only daily that operated without interruption throughout the crisis.

Even so, Freneau did have an impact. He poked fun at those who fled the city, at the power of opium to banish pain, and at the cruelty and indifference of those outside the city. His weapons of choice were brief dialogues and verse. The construction of his verse was often clumsy, possibly because strict deadlines meant he had to work so quickly.

He did manage to catch a vivid sense of the plague in one memorable poem called "Pestilence."

Hot dry winds forever blowing,
Dead men to the grave-yards going:
Constant hearses,
Funeral verses;
Oh! What plagues—there is no knowing!

Priests retreating from their pulpits!—
Some in hot, and some in cold fits
In bad temper,
Off they scamper,
Leaving us—unhappy culprits!

Doctors raving and disputing,
Death's pale army still recruiting—
What a pother
One with t'other!
Some a-writing, some a-shooting.

Nature's poisons here collected,
Water, earth, and air infected—
O, what pity,
Such a City,
Was in such a place erected!

Humor might relieve the tension, but only for a few minutes. In time, the reader would look up and see the deserted streets, hear some nearby cry for help. The horror was all around and not likely to go away soon.

During this sad, helpless time, another bit of verse appeared outside Woodstown, New Jersey. Major Christian Piercy had fled Philadelphia after his son and an apprentice caught the fever, bribing a stagecoach driver to take him and his family to south Jersey.

Piercy grew ill on the ride out of Camden, and the other passengers—including those from his household—put him out of the coach at Isaac Eldridge's farm. Eldridge would not allow the sick man in his house, but he did let Piercy stay in an abandoned log cabin in the woods. There Piercy died and was buried without ceremony where he had fallen. Later his family had a headstone put in place that bore this warning verse:

> *Stay Passenger see where I lie*
> *As you are now so once was I*
> *As I am now so You shall be*
> *Prepare for Death and follow me.*

William Hercules, ſhoemaker
Elizabeth Herleman
George Herman, baker
George Herlemin
William Herman's wife
William Hertzog, labourer
Chriſtopher Herrely, labourer
John Herrill
Wife of Nicholas Heſs, black-ſmith
George Heſs's ſiſter
Iſaac Heſton
—— Hetnick, baker
Iſrael Hewlings, ſhoemaker
Joſeph Hewlings, bricklayer
Henry Hewmes, copperſmith
John Huſon, ſailor
Mrs. Hewit
Andrew Hews
John Heyberger, jun.
Mary Heyberger
John Heyburn
Andrew Heyd's ſon
Benja. Hickman's wife & ſon
David Hickman, clerk
Joſeph Hicks, gluemaker
John Hicks
Richard Hicks
John Hierſon, hatter
William Hickert's wife
John Jacob Hiertman, malſter
Angel Higgenbottom
William Higgenbottom
Joſeph Higgins
Mary Hightſon
Suſannah Higgin, widow
Martin Hilderburn, ſieve-maker
Wife of George Hill, clerk
Robert Hill
Wife of Jacob Hill, fiſherman
James Hill, bricklayer
James Hill, clerk
John Hill, chair-maker
Johannah Hill, jun.
John Hill's daughter
Samuel Hill, Ir.
James Hillman, apprentice
Jacob Hillman, blackſmith
Catharine Hillner
Jacob Hilſinger, labourer
William Hiltzheimer
Mary Hinan
George Hinckel, watchman
John Hinckel's ſon
Chriſtop'r Hineman's daughter
Jane Hiltridge
George Hinton, cutler
Mrs. Hirſt
Mary Hirrine
George Hiſhatters
Samuel Hampton's ſon
Henry Haare, cardmaker
John Hobſon, ſievemaker
Barbara Hackenſoffe
John Hockley, ironmonger
Elizabeth Hobſon
Jeffrey Hadnet, ſadler, and ſon
Chriſtopher Hocknoble
Catharine Hoff
Catharine Hoffman
Regina Hoffman
Iſaac Hoffman, ſailor
Henry Hoffman, baker
Suſanna Hoffman
Jacob Hoffner, ſchoolmaſter, Germ.
Philip Hofner, carter
Michael Hoft's ſon
Edward Hogan's two children
Dr. Hodge's child
Andrew Hodge's child
Joſeph Hogg, carpenter, of New-Jerſey
Anna Catharina Hefflein
Jacob Holberſtadt, labourer
Charles Hold, hatter
Benjamin Holden, maſon
Charles Holden
Wm. Holderneſſe's ſon Thomas
Samuel Holgate
William Holklow
Barbara Hollard, widow
Philip Hollard, cooper
John Holmes, farmer
Sarah Holmes, widow
Sar ah
Thomas Holmes's wife
Moſes Homberg, innkeeper
George Honigs
William Honck, wife and child, turner
Chriſtopher Honey
John Honecker and wife

CHAPTER NINE

"A Delicate Situation"

It gives great pleasure to the Editor to hear, from every quarter of our City, that universal health prevails in a degree equal to any former period.

—*The Federal Gazette*, November 1, 1793

Monday, October 28. George Washington had been impatient since his departure from Philadelphia in early September. When he left the stricken city, he had put Secretary of War Henry Knox in charge of the government, giving the former general clear instructions to report to him weekly concerning the spread of yellow fever. But after a few days' close contact with the pestilence, Knox found that his warrior instinct had abandoned him. He closed up his house and fled across New Jersey to Manhattan Island.

Knox was turned away from Manhattan and wound up in Elizabethtown, New Jersey, where he spent two weeks in quarantine. He did write to Washington, telling the president that the militia was out all over New Jersey hunting for fever victims, and that Manhattan was in a state of panic over the possibility that the fever would visit there. But he provided no useful information about the fever in Philadelphia.

Opposite: *From Mathew Carey's list of the dead, 1794.*
(The Library Company of Philadelphia)

Washington's own efforts to find out what was going on did not produce satisfying results, either, especially for a man who wanted to be kept informed about all matters. "I would thank you for precise information on this head, for I have not been able to get any," he wrote to the comptroller of the treasury, Oliver Wolcott.

Wolcott was one of only three high-ranking officials of the federal government within a day's ride of Philadelphia, Attorney General Edmund Randolph and Postmaster General Timothy Pickering being the others. But these men were struggling to keep their departments functioning and had little spare time to gather information or write reports, even for the leader of the country.

The few pieces of information the president did obtain were often second- or thirdhand and usually vague in nature. "The accounts we receive here," he lamented, "are so opposite and unsatisfactory that we know not on what to rely." It was, Washington complained, "a delicate situation for the President to be placed in."

Adding to his frustration was the fact that very few official papers had made their way to him at Mount Vernon. Washington was a stickler for orderly files that he could search at a moment's notice. This was the most important way he kept himself informed about the hundreds of things happening in the fledgling nation. Unfortunately, when the government clerks had panicked and dashed from Philadelphia, they had abandoned all papers and records in boarded-up houses. No one knew where these documents were; and no one was willing to risk his or her life wandering through the infected city in search of them.

Washington did his best to answer questions and make decisions, but he often found his efforts blocked. At one point Thomas Sim Lee, the governor of Maryland, wanted to know what he should do with the British ship *Roehampton,* which had been seized by one of Genêt's hired privateers and brought into Baltimore Harbor. The British were upset over the seizure, and wanted their ship back, while the French were upset that the ship was being detained until the president could decide what to do.

A very embarrassed George Washington finally had to confess to Lee, "I brought no public papers of any sort (not even the rules which have been established in these cases,) along with me; consequently am not prepared at this place to decide points which may require a reference to papers not within my reach."

To make matters worse for Washington, the question about whether he could legally call Congress into session outside Philadelphia was still very much up in the air. He had sought advice on the issue from a number of cabinet members and government officials, but no agreement had been reached.

Alexander Hamilton felt the president could indeed move Congress. After all, Hamilton reasoned, the government would not automatically cease functioning if an enemy army captured the capital. Why wouldn't the same principle apply in the case of a devastating natural disaster, such as a plague?

But Thomas Jefferson and James Madison disagreed and could not be budged from their position. During the formation of the federal government, they argued, individual states had been extremely wary about giving away too much of their governing power to any future president. Their nervousness was the result of British history.

English kings had allowed their subjects to participate in making laws through representatives in Parliament. This system of government worked as long as the king was not challenged on important matters. Whenever the Parliament clashed with their monarch, the king would get his way by suddenly convening Parliament in a remote, unreachable part of the country. Without a proper quorum of members, the king could then decide law as he pleased.

As a result, representatives in the United States had drawn up the Constitution with particular attention to the issue of where they would meet in the future. As far as Jefferson and Madison were concerned, only Congress could relocate itself, and it could do this only after it officially convened in Philadelphia.

Finally, Washington turned to Attorney General Edmund Randolph. As the nation's chief law official and legal counsel of the United States, Randolph was someone whose opinion held great weight. In a delicately worded letter, Randolph told Washington that no, the president could not move Congress, even in an emergency. "It seems to be unconstitutional," Randolph noted. If the federal government was to continue to operate, then Congress would have to meet in Philadelphia, whether or not the deadly fever was still present.

Toward the end of October, Washington heard from Postmaster General Pickering that the fever seemed to be on the wane. A cold spell had swept in and with it a cleansing rain. Burials were falling in number, from a high of 120 on October 11 to half that number on October 21.

This good news was followed almost immediately by a contradictory report from Comptroller Wolcott. After several good days in the city, he explained, warm weather reappeared and deaths increased, jumping to 82 on October 22. Wolcott advised the president to delay his return trip several more days.

Clearly, the city was not yet safe.

This didn't please the anxious president, who had already been out of touch with critically important matters for over six weeks. He could write back and ask again what was happening in the city, but this would take an unbearable amount of time. Before the fever, a letter could travel by fast post from his home to the city and a reply be received in three to six days. Now letters to and from Philadelphia had to undergo special processing, such as being dipped in vinegar and allowed to dry. It was taking mail anywhere from ten days to two weeks to make the journey these days! Further delay was out of the question.

George and Martha Washington, along with two young relatives and a servant, at Mount Vernon in Virginia. (The Historical Society of Pennsylvania)

On October 28, Washington climbed aboard a coach and headed north, accompanied by Tobias Lear and a valet. The president described his five-day trip in one simple, businesslike sentence: "Set out from Mount Vernon the 28 October & arrived at Germantown the 1st. of Novemr."

Thomas Jefferson was also returning to the Philadelphia area to complete his time as secretary of state. He joined up with Washington in Baltimore. Unlike the president, Jefferson had a great deal to say about his journey—about the heat, rain, dust, and expense. Because no coaches were running north of Baltimore, the president and his secretary of state were forced to hire—at their own expense, Jefferson grumped—a carriage to take them to Germantown. All along the way

Jefferson chafed at the jump in prices brought about by "harpies who prey upon travelers" returning to Philadelphia. Inns on the route had upped their rates; ferrymen were charging extra to transport people and carriages across rivers. In the end, Jefferson estimated that it cost him nearly eighty dollars just to get to Germantown.

His annoyance continued even after he reached his destination. The seven inns around the village were still jammed with folk who had left Philadelphia, and the few larger houses in the area were already filled with guests. By prior arrangement Washington went to stay at the elegant and comfortable home of David Deshler. Jefferson, on the other hand, had to beg the proprietor of the King of Prussia Tavern for a place to sleep. Even then he did not get a furnished room. "We must give from 4 to 6 to 8 dollars a week," he complained, "for [a closet] without a bed . . . a chair or table."

Jefferson did well to find a private space, as cramped and bare as it was. Two congressmen and future presidents, James Madison and James Monroe, would arrive after him and be compelled to sleep on wooden benches in the tavern's public room!

What Washington and the others discovered was that, despite the surge in deaths on October 22, the fever did indeed seem to be losing strength. Deaths fell to below thirty on Saturday, October 26. Dr. Benjamin Rush looked about his neighborhood that day and found that there was not a single person ill on his block. "The disease visibly and universally declines," he wrote to Julia, his confidence returning.

Elizabeth Drinker opened her front door to find "a delightful, cool, frosty morning," adding, "'Tis generally agreed that the fever is very much abated."

The committee, meanwhile, noted a lessening in demands for their assistance and passed a resolution saying: "It [has] pleased Divine Providence to favor us with an agreeable prospect of returning health to our long afflicted city." The fever wasn't completely gone, the committee was quick to confess, but it would be safe for "our fugitive brethren" to return in a week to ten days.

People who had hidden themselves indoors began to emerge and walk the streets again. Shop doors opened for business, and ships once again sailed upriver to discharge cargo; farmers arrived, their wagons loaded with provisions bound for the markets of a very hungry city. Plans were even announced for the resumption of the stagecoach in early November. The city seemed to be awakening after a long, inescapable nightmare. Andrew Brown, the editor of *The Federal Gazette,* devoted an optimistic paragraph to the "dawn of returning health and order."

Most doctors had predicted the fever would end when the cold weather returned. Almost all epidemics followed the same pattern, striking during warm weather, disappearing with the first hard frost. Daniel Defoe, in recording the end of the Black Death that visited London in 1665, wrote that "the winter weather came on apace [and] most of those that had fallen sick recovered, and the health of the city began to return."

The same was true for Philadelphia in 1793. The number of deaths would go above twenty only twice after October 27. Those who had escaped the city began to trickle back home. "Every hour," Mathew Carey observed with relief, "long-absent and welcome faces appear."

Those returning found their city a changed place. The streets were remarkably clean, for one thing. The trash and garbage had been swept away; dead animals—cats, dogs, birds, and pigs—had been removed. Gone, too, were the beggars and homeless children.

Most changed of all were those who had been left behind. The survivors were exhausted and haggard looking, their clothes frayed and soiled and smelling heavily of vinegar and camphor. The skin of many

ice,
ued
the
iat-
it,
jor
1.
Su-
Fort
A,
sfac-
nost
ſent
this
etter
and
opes
and
ls of
n or
tate.
r,
3.
with
the
con-
t the
alth,
ually
es in
s; &
that
of it
days.
hoſ-
Of
nain
hen-
the
r ci-
/, it
hath
their
have
tiga-
e diſ-
ſſary
com-
hem
nd to
the
/.
y or
of by
thoſe
would

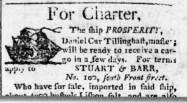

Wm. ALLEN, Deputy
Health-Officer.

I DO further certify, that in conſequence of an alarm among the citizens, ariſing from a report, that a malignant fever was very prevalent among the people on board, I viſited the abovementioned ſhip, Citizen of Marſeilles, yeſterday, the 11th inſt. and was happy in meeting on board, Doctor Deveze, the very reſpectable French Phyſician, who has lately rendered ſuch eſſential ſervices to the committee of ſick, by his attendance at the hoſpital at Buſh-Hill. —Dr. Deveze was ſo obliging as to accompany me to the governor's, where we fortunately met a committee of the merchants, before whom, I reported to the governor, that I had that day viſited the ſhip a ſecond time, where I found the wounded as before. But that there was not one perſon on board appearing to be affected at all with any thing malignant or dangerous to the health of the citizens; and Dr. Deveze confirmed the ſame in the moſt explicit and unequivocal manner.

SAMUEL DUFFIELD.

Nov. 12, 1793.

BY THIS DAY'S MAIL.

NEW-YORK, November 12.

Intelligence From Oſtend.

Citizen Bonne, quarter-maſter of the artillery of the national battalion of Finiſtere, arrived this morning at the French Miniſter's from Oſtend, where he had been taken priſoner, and from whence he departed on the 12th of September, on board the American veſſel the Young Eagle, which touched at New-London the 8th inſt. This officer brings the confirmation of the total rout of the army of the Duke of York, whoſe loſs was eſtimated at Oſtend at 6000 men, according to the moſt moderate computation.

His eyes were bleſſed with the ſight of the French emigrants limping along, who had begun the flight, and whom the Engliſh grenadiers and dragoons were curſing moſt heartily. He ſaw Prince Erneſt Adolphus carried on a litter dangerouſly wounded, Three Britiſh Generals fell on the field of battle, and all the artillery was abandoned to the French.

This glorious ſucceſs muſt have been followed by another in the ſame quarter; 45,000 men detached from the army of the Moſelle were in full march, evidently with an intention to block up the wreck of the combined armies, in conjunction with the troops encamped near Liſle and Caſſel.

There was as yet no intelligence of the other armies of the Republic, but it was generally known, that on the ſame day they had all diſplayed the moſt vigorous efforts to cruſh the baſe enemies of the French people. The rebels of La Vendee were entirely defeated. The

By Authority.

Pennſylvania, ſſ.

By THOMAS MIFFLIN,

Governor of the Commonwealth of Pennſylvania.

A Proclamation,

Appointing a day of general Humiliation, Thankſgiving and Prayer.

WHEREAS it hath pleaſed Almighty GOD to put an end to the grievous Calamity, that recently afflicted the City of Philadelphia; and it is the Duty of all, who are truly ſenſible of the Divine Juſtice and Mercy, to employ the earlieſt moments of returning Health, in devout expreſſions of penitence, ſubmiſſion, and gratitude: THEREFORE I have deemed it proper to iſſue this Proclamation; hereby appointing THURSDAY, the *Twelfth Day of December* next, to be holden throughout the Commonwealth, as a Day of general Humiliation, Thankſgiving, and Prayer. AND I earneſtly exhort and entreat my Fellow-Citizens, to abſtain on that Day from all their worldly Avocations; and to unite in Confeſſing, with contrite Hearts, our manifold ſins and tranſgreſſions; in acknowledging, with thankful adoration, the mercy and goodneſs of the Supreme Ruler and Preſerver of the Univerſe,—more eſpecially manifeſted in our late deliverance; and in praying, with ſolemn zeal, that the ſame mighty Power would be graciouſly pleaſed to inſtil into our Minds the juſt principles of our duty to Him, and to our Fellow Creatures;—to regulate and guide all our actions by his Holy Spirit:—to avert from all Mankind the evils of War, Peſtilence and Famine;—and to bleſs and protect us in the enjoyment of Civil and Religious Liberty. AND all officers of the Commonwealth, as well as all Paſtors and Teachers, are, alſo, particularly requeſted to make known this Proclamation, and, by their example and advice, to recommend a punctual obſervance thereof, within their reſpective juriſdictions and congregations:—ſo that the voice of the People, ſtrengthened by its unanimity, and ſanctified by ſincerity, aſcending to the Throne of Grace, may there find favor and acceptance.

GIVEN *under my Hand and the Great Seal of the State, at Philadelphia, this Fourteenth Day of November, in the Year of our LORD one Thouſand ſeven Hundred and ninety Three, and of the Independence of America the eighteenth.*

THOMAS MIFFLIN.

By the Governor:

A. J. DALLAS, Secretary of the Commonwealth.

who had gotten the fever retained a sickly yellow glow. Those who had taken the mercury purge were constantly spitting to rid their mouths of the foul taste the drug left behind. When they smiled, their teeth were stained an unsightly black.

These reminders of the yellow fever did not shake the spirit of optimism that gripped the city. Rayner Taylor announced that he would be printing "an anthem suitable to the present occasion." Thomas Boylston Adams, son of Vice President John Adams, wrote to his nervous parents in Quincy, Massachusetts, "The idea of danger is dissipated in a moment when we perceive thousands walking in perfect security about their customary business, & no ill consequences ensuing from it." On the very last day of October, a huge white flag was hoisted at Bush Hill that proclaimed: NO MORE SICK PERSONS HERE.

The fever was gone, folk around town declared happily.

And then, even in defiance of the cold weather and a dusting of snow, several of the recently returned residents developed symptoms of the disease. A silversmith known only as Mr. Brooks reopened his shop on October 31 and was dead of yellow fever on November 3. Others fell ill as well. While these new incidences of yellow fever were few and scattered, they demonstrated clearly that the disease had not been completely wiped out. It still lurked in dark, unclean corners, still clung to dirty sheets and curtains.

Once again the carts carried the sick to Bush Hill, and the white flag of victory had to be hauled down. The committee issued a public warning, telling recent arrivals to clean their homes thoroughly, burn gunpowder to purify the air, dump lime down their privies, and whitewash every room.

OPPOSITE: *Governor Mifflin's proclamation (along with other news and ads), as it appeared in the November 14 edition of* The Federal Gazette.

(THE LIBRARY COMPANY OF PHILADELPHIA)

A typical day along Arch Street at the close of the eighteenth century.

(The Historical Society of Pennsylvania)

The reemergence of the deadly disease did not stop people from returning to the city. It did, however, leave a lingering sense of helplessness. Well into December, individuals were still succumbing to the fever, and Thomas Jefferson was worrying over which houses were safe to enter. "Yellow fever," he predicted, "will discourage the growth of great cities in the nation."

One of the last diary entries Elizabeth Drinker made concerning the plague spoke of the unshakable unease the invisible killer had left in its wake. "M. D. observed, while at her sister's this afternoon, a Coffin, a cart, and 10 or 12 persons walking on ye pavement as attendants. 'Tis to be feared that ye Yellow Fever is not entirely over."

On Sunday morning, November 10, George Washington mounted his horse and rode out of Germantown without bothering to wake his aides. Tired of not knowing the true condition of Philadelphia and frustrated by the general nervousness of everyone around him, Washington took it upon himself to make an inspection.

Down the five miles Washington traveled, through forests and past scattered farmhouses and fields, over the small bridge covering Pegg Run, until he entered the city. He spent the next while riding up one street and down another, nodding politely to the few people he happened to encounter at that early hour. The air smelled fine; the streets were clean and orderly. Aside from the tiny red flags stuck on houses, there was no outward sign of the fever anywhere.

He rode back to Germantown later that day to tell his shocked staff where he'd been. Best of all, he informed them, the nation's capital was healthy enough for Congress to meet there in December, as planned.

The city filled up again and took on its normal, preplague pace. The markets bustled with activity; the taverns and coffeehouses buzzed with conversation; the federal, state, and local governments took up the business they had left off in September.

Benjamin Rush emerged from the epidemic emaciated, feeble, and haunted. In a letter to Julia, he expressed what was probably on the minds of many of those who had stayed and survived. "Sometimes seated in your easy chair by the fire," he wrote, "I lose myself in looking back upon the ocean which I have passed, and now and then find myself surprised by a tear in reflecting upon the friends I have lost, and the scenes of distress that I have witnessed, and which I was unable to relieve."

No one would ever know precisely how many Philadelphians died of yellow fever in 1793. Many of those who traditionally kept such count—ministers, sextons, and city officials—had either fled the city or been ill themselves. The best estimates put the number of victims at between four and five thousand men, women, and children. What was clear to all was that life would never be the same. The fear had gone too deep, the losses were all too real and personal.

Widow Morrison's child
William Morrison
John Morrow, jun. gunsmith
Mrs. ——— Morrow
Rosina Morrow
Alexander Mortimer, gardener
Deborah Morton
John Morton and apprentice
Christian Moser
Mary Moss
Marquis Monbrun
Philip Mountree, brewer
Wife of Nicholas Muff, harness-maker
Ann Mullen, mantua-maker
Catharine Mullen
Edward Mullen
James Mullen, hatter
James Mullen's wife
John Mullen, chairmaker
Mary Mullen
Michael Mullen's two children
Patrick Mullen
Robert Mullen, house-carpenter, and apprentice
James Mullener, apprentice
Edmund Mullery, grocer
James Mumford, blacksmith
Major Henry Mumford
Rachel Mumford
Child of Robert Murdoch, labourer
Sarah Murdoch
—— Murley
Ann Murphy
John Murphy, black-smith
Mary Murphy
Michael Murphy's daughter
Richard Murphy
Susannah Murphy
Timothy Murphy
Margaret Murthwaite
Mary Murthwaite
Rev. Alexander Murray, D. D.
Eleanor Murray
James Murray, shoemaker, Ir.
Robert Murray's wife and child
Sarah Murray
William Murray
Mrs. ——— Musketts
Rebecca Musgrove, a stranger
Widow Musterholt
Adam Myers, baker
Catharine Myers
Hannah Myers, servant
Margaret Myers
Henry Myers, hair-dresser
John Myers's child
Margaret Myers
Michael Myers
Michael Mynick
Sophia Mynick
Adam Myon, labourer
John Myrietta
Jac. Mytinger, tavern-keeper, and wife
Henry Nagle's mother-in-law
Mary Nagle
Hannah Nailor
John Nailor
Samuel Napp
William Nash, baker
Lewis Nass, blacksmith
——— Navarre
Thomas Nave's wife
Thomas Near
Israel Nedham, skinner, Engl.
Robert Neeley, sailor
Tho. Neeves, carpenter, & wife
Margaret Neil
Wife and girl of Andrew Nielson, tavern-keeper
George Niess, shoemaker
Benedict Nesmos, son, & daugh.
Elizabeth Neman
Thomas Nemerson
Timmons Nevil
Elizabeth New
Anthony Newingham
John Newling, a lad
Elizabeth Newman
Fred. Newman's wife & child
Susannah Newman
Forbes Newton's wife
Margaret Nibley
Magnus Nice, oyster-man
Martha Nichols, spinster, Æt. 70
Wm. Nichols, Æt. 73
Mary Nichols, wife of ditto
Wm. Nichols, wheelwright, and wife
Thomas Nicholson, joiner
John Nick
Augustus Niel
Jane, daughter of Wm. Niles
Elizabeth Noble
Catharine Nodler
Anthony Noll, ropemaker

CHAPTER TEN

Improvements and the Public Gratitude

An ill name is easier given than taken away.

—ABSALOM JONES AND RICHARD ALLEN, JANUARY 1794

Wednesday, January 8, 1794. "If the disease has disappeared as it no doubt has," wrote "Howard" in that day's *General Advertiser,* "every memento of its existence should disappear with it, that the citizens may once more enjoy repose."

No doubt some people agreed with "Howard." The danger was gone, they said, so let's forget about it completely and get back to business and life as it was before yellow fever's visit. This was an especially strong wish among the fugitives, who were embarrassed at having abandoned their city in its time of great need.

Charles Biddle, for instance, tried to ignore the entire tragedy by insisting that those who had died were all foreign-born or strangers to the city. When asked about a dead friend who had been born and raised in the United States, Biddle explained that he hadn't really died of the fever. He had actually been "frightened to death."

OPPOSITE: *From Mathew Carey's list of the dead, 1794.*
(THE LIBRARY COMPANY OF PHILADELPHIA)

Biddle and those who thought as he did were the exceptions. Most people, like it or not, had had their lives changed too profoundly by the fever to make believe it hadn't happened.

Take the case of Dolley Payne Todd. She had lost her adoring husband, John, and a newborn baby son to the fever; and even though she had removed herself and her two-year-old son to a farm at Gray's Ferry, they had both become infected and been close to death themselves. Even so, Dolley returned with her mother and son to her pleasant brick home on Fourth and Walnut Streets in November and began taking in gentleman boarders to pay her bills.

This drawing of Dolley Madison was done a few years after she married James Madison and moved to the nation's new capital in Washington, D.C.

(THE HISTORICAL SOCIETY OF PENNSYLVANIA)

Dolley was no wallflower, content to spend the rest of her days living in the past. She was too intelligent, lively, and attractive for such a passive existence. Eleven months after John Todd's death, Dolley married a congressman from Virginia named James Madison. The yellow fever certainly had a tragic impact on her life, one she would recall often in the years to come; yet it was out of this that Dolley Madison's role in our nation's history—as hostess for the widower president Thomas Jefferson and then first lady for her husband—was born.

Government also found itself changed. The Pennsylvania legislature realized that the state government had ceased to exist when its members scampered from the city in panic. They never admitted personal failure or cowardice; to do so might be used against them in coming elections. Instead, they factored flight into the structure of the state government; in the event that yellow fever or any other natural disaster might rout them again, they gave the governor special authority to make laws and spend money until the crisis ended.

The national government learned something because of the yellow fever epidemic as well. The states had worried so much about a future autocratic president that the federal government had inadvertently created a constitutional crisis for the one currently in office. To avoid repeating such an awkward and embarrassing situation, Congress passed a law giving the president power to call it into session outside of the nation's capital whenever a grave hazard to life and health existed.

Changes also came to the city because of the fever. While no one knew what caused yellow fever, the doctors agreed that foul smells were not healthy and might promote disease. Therefore, efforts were made to keep the markets and streets free of offensive-smelling matter, and the laws holding homeowners responsible for cleaning up their property were strengthened. At first, these laws were rather weak and generally ignored by all. But as the nineteenth century went along and the link between filth and disease became more apparent, public health codes were strengthened and enforced.

That the poorer areas of Philadelphia—those mean, narrow alleys with their run-down, airless houses—had suffered the worst did not escape attention. However, no municipal works projects—such as putting in a sewer system to eliminate the polluted "sinks"—were initiated to change the wretched conditions. There was no money whatsoever in the city's budget for such costly endeavors, plus no desire to undertake them. Holding down city expenditures was deemed more important at the time than public health. Instead, when the fever rampaged through Philadelphia in summers to come, vast tent encampments were erected for the poor by the Schuylkill River and in the Northern Liberties. Poor

As the city gradually got back to normal, people once again strolled along the tree-lined paths behind the state house. (THE LIBRARY COMPANY OF PHILADELPHIA)

people couldn't flee to comfortable country homes like their wealthier neighbors, but at least they could escape the most squalid and plague-ridden sections of town.

The biggest improvement was made in the way water was supplied to Philadelphia. In 1793 water for drinking, cooking, cleaning, and putting out fires all came from private and public wells or from the Delaware River. Most wells were dug in the cellars or backyards of homes, usually only a few feet away from the privy pit. In addition to human waste, the byproducts from manufacturers, such as tanneries, and refuse from the markets seeped into the drinking water. As for the Delaware, it was a handy dumping ground for anything and everything—household and human waste, manufacturing rubbish, and debris from the hundreds of ships that visited the city every year. The result was evil-smelling and evil-tasting water.

While the College of Physicians assured everyone that yellow fever did not originate in the water, the majority of citizens felt otherwise. If the foul smell of rotting coffee could cause health problems, they reasoned, why couldn't foul-smelling water? Complaints about the water and its link to yellow fever increased with each new visitation, until action was finally taken in 1799. That was when the city hired Benjamin Latrobe to design and construct Philadelphia's first waterworks.

Water was lifted by a steam-engine pump from the Schuylkill River (which was then purer than the Delaware) and forced along a tunnel to the central pump house, located in the large central square at Broad and High Streets, just two blocks from Ricketts' Circus. There another steam-engine pump lifted the water into huge wood reservoirs, from where it was fed by gravity to households and businesses around the city.

Water from the system—the first water system in the United States—was sweeter tasting and had no offensive odor. Plus the water

The large central square where the holding tank of the waterworks was constructed became a popular place to visit and have picnics. (THE LIBRARY COMPANY OF PHILADELPHIA)

flowed with enough force to hose streets and docks clean and to flush open clogged sewers. Eliminating the backbreaking need to hand-pump every drop of water had another beneficial effect as well. People began to bathe more often. Elizabeth Drinker took a bath in 1799, a full twenty-eight years after her previous bath!

Even President Washington learned a valuable lesson as a result of his encounter with yellow fever. The president had enjoyed his stay at David Deshler's comfortable, rambling home in Germantown during the autumn of 1793. When yellow fever returned to Philadelphia the next summer, Washington wasted no time in removing Martha, himself, and the rest of his household—along with his official papers!—to that safe location again. This became the nation's first "summer White House," and presidents ever since have followed the tradition by establishing their own warm-weather residences.

As for Washington's French problem, the fever had an impact on it as well. Genêt had fled Philadelphia and its epidemic for Manhattan in September, but the passions surrounding him and the Neutrality Act seemed to have died along the way. His reception in Manhattan was tepid; meanwhile, his supporters in Philadelphia had their minds on survival, not politics. In time, the French government, prompted by complaints from the United States, replaced Genêt with a new minister, who brought along orders for Genêt's arrest. The tensions between the United States and France would linger for years, but the immediate crisis ended. Years later John Adams would recall the street riots outside George Washington's residence: "The coolest and the firmest minds . . . have given their opinion to me, that nothing but the yellow fever . . . could have saved the United States from a total revolution of government."

No, the memory of the yellow fever wouldn't disappear as easily as "Howard" demanded. Besides, some people just wouldn't let it fade from their memory. The doctors, for instance, were still disputing. One of the first things Governor Mifflin did when he returned in late October was to ask the College of Physicians to write a report concerning the cause of the disease.

As requested, the College assembled, but the veneer of mutual respect and consideration had worn very thin. Physicians had been forced to take sides during the fever when the squabbles hit the newspapers; they came to the meeting with their opinions fixed. Instead of a careful discussion of the disease, the physicians bickered and fought.

The doctors holding that the fever had been imported won out simply because there were more of them. To the delight of Governor Mifflin and Philadelphia businessmen, the College declared: "No instance has ever occurred of the disease called yellow fever, having originated in this city, or in any other parts of the United States."

Rush was incensed at what he viewed as flawed medical logic and professional jealousy—and promptly resigned from the College of

Physicians. One of the few doctors who had not quarreled with Rush tried to persuade him to reconsider: "Oh, my friend," wrote Dr. Samuel Griffitts, "search & see if our Resentments are to make us quit places where we can be eminently useful."

But Rush's mind was made up, and everyone knew what that meant. He would not back down. In fact, he was seriously thinking of leaving Philadelphia and the practice of medicine altogether. "The envy and hatred of my brethren has lately risen to a rage," Rush explained. "They blush at their mistakes, they feel for their murders, and instead of asking forgiveness of the public for them, vent all of their guilty shame and madness upon the man who convicted them of both."

In the end, Rush stayed in the city and reestablished a strong medical practice (though he never attended another gathering at the College). But the controversy persisted. Many doctors took up the pen in order to write about their experiences during the plague, as well as to argue in support of whichever treatment they favored. And so from the pages of the newspapers to the pages of books the accusations and name-calling raged on.

Actually, the writing began long before the deadly fever disappeared. Dr. William Currie's sixty-four-page *A Description of the Malignant, Infectious Fever Prevailing at Present in Philadelphia* appeared at the beginning of September, when the fever was confined to a few streets and alleys. It was the first book on Philadelphia's plague, and while Currie did not call it yellow fever, his description of the fever's symptoms is detailed and accurate. Other physicians followed Currie's lead, with David Nassy, Jean Devèze, Isaac Cathrall, Nathaniel Potter, and, of course, Benjamin Rush publishing books in the weeks and years to come.

The entire controversy reerupted whenever yellow fever appeared again in the city, as it did in 1794, 1796, 1797, and 1798. Rush bled and purged aggressively and argued for his cure each time; other doctors hotly argued against it and him. In 1797 Rush's opponents were joined by a new and highly virulent voice—that of journalist William Cobbett.

Cobbett was an Englishman who had been driven from his homeland because of his attacks on corruption in the English army. He despised those American colonials who had fought against his England,

William Cobbett certainly doesn't seem to be a nasty, vengeful man as he lounges in his parlor chair. (The Historical Society of Pennsylvania)

yet he still chose to settle in Philadelphia, where he set up a royalist newspaper called *The Porcupine's Gazette.*

Cobbett hated Rush because of Rush's prominent connection to the Revolution and his belief in representative government. "He has long, very long, been sedulously employed in scuffling up his little hillock of fame. I will down him," Cobbett promised, then attacked Rush in prose and verse in just about every issue of his paper. "Blood, blood, still they cry, more blood!" he wrote about Rush and his followers. "In every sentence they menace our poor veins. Their language is as frightful to the ears of the alarmed multitude as the raven's croak to those of the sickly flock."

Even in an era when newspapers often attacked political enemies ruthlessly, Cobbett's attacks were particularly vicious and personal. He called Rush a quack and a murderer, and even suggested the doctor was mentally unstable. Before the yellow fever epidemic, even the doctors who disagreed with Rush on medical matters would have defended him against Cobbett's irrational assaults. But the infighting had taken such a nasty turn during the fever—thanks largely to Rush's aggressive personality—that he was forced to defend himself on his own.

Rush stood the abuse for as long as possible, then moved to Princeton to find some peace. Cobbett continued his anti-Rush ravings anyway. When Rush applied for a position at the medical faculty of Columbia University in New York City, his appointment was blocked by another enemy of his cure, Alexander Hamilton.

Rush once again vowed to retire, but decided to regain his good name before doing so. He sued Cobbett for libel, and after a long and public trial in 1800, the jury awarded Rush $5,000, plus $3,000 court costs. Instead of paying, Cobbett fled Philadelphia and then the country. Some of Cobbett's personal possessions were sold, and Rush donated the money to charity. The victory was enough to lure him from retirement a second time, but his reputation was forever tarnished. He spent the remaining thirteen years of his life curing diseases and battling opponents with his customary stubborn ferocity.

Many of Philadelphia's most pious citizens would not let the fever disappear entirely, either. This group included Elhanan Winchester, Samuel Stearns, and the Reverend J. Henry C. Helmuth. The terrible visitation, they argued, had been a warning from the Almighty to mend the city's spiritual ways. Samuel Stearns summed up their feelings in a bit of awkward verse: "This *mortal* Plague at thy command / And thou thereby hast *humbled* sinful man!"

These spiritual guardians were shocked when people in Philadelphia ignored the obvious lessons and began living as they had before the visitation. "How soon after were the play-houses opened and other scenes of amusement!" Winchester noted with disgust, adding a warning, "I tell you, except ye repent, ye shall all likewise perish."

Numerous citizens agreed with such alarming views, but certainly not a majority of the people. Most knew in their hearts that they would never completely forget the terrible weeks when illness had taken hold of their city and killed friends and family members. But they weren't about to blame themselves for the tragedy.

What happened to the heroes of the epidemic?

Those on the committee received due praise from the returning council members and from the state legislature, but voices of criticism were also heard. In December anonymous letter writers to *The Federal Gazette* condemned the committee members for seizing power so arrogantly. "The bulk of them," one critic said disparagingly, "are scarcely known beyond the smoke of their own chimnies."

The committee counted up the money it had spent and subtracted the many donations that had come in from cities like New York, Baltimore, and Boston: it had spent $3,245.12 more than it had taken in. This deficit remained the personal responsibility of the members of the committee, with chair maker John Letchworth required to pay a little over one pound (a substantial sum at that time) as his share. Most likely, the few wealthier members of the committee, such as Matthew Clarkson, Stephen Girard, and Israel Israel, shouldered the greatest part of the debt. After this, most committee members simply went back to their old occupations, happy to give up the positions of power they had held during the terrible time of death and sickness.

Israel Israel did not choose to step aside and let the workings of the city government continue as usual. He ran for the Pennsylvania state legislature three times, in 1793, 1795, and 1797. Each time his campaign stressed his commitment to the poor and the fact that the government in Philadelphia was controlled by a wealthy few who tended to disregard the welfare of its less fortunate citizens. Hire more scavengers to clean up the tiny and forgotten alleys, he recommended. Pave the streets and put in sewers to drain off excess water.

Israel lost in his first two bids. But the vote for the third election happened during the 1797 recurrence of yellow fever, when most well-to-do citizens had left the city. Israel won that election by a slim margin of 38 votes out of 4,010 cast.

His opponent, Benjamin R. Morgan, denounced the results, saying the fever had driven "respectable inhabitants" out of town. Morgan petitioned the state senate, arguing that Israel's election was illegal because people from the two poorest sections of town had been allowed to vote without proving they had taken an oath of allegiance. The oath had been instituted by the state after the Revolutionary War to weed out anyone who might want to see the British back in power; although the law remained on the books, taking the oath had not been a voting requirement since 1790. But that didn't matter to the senate. It ordered a reelection at the end of February 1798.

Needless to say, the reelection became a war of words in the newspapers. A backer of Israel who called himself "A Friend of Justice" argued that if the oath were uniformly required, not a single legislator could claim to be legally elected. Another signed his name as "A Republican" and said Israel's election had been put aside only because he was a "zealous defender of, and advocate for liberty and equality amongst men, disapproving of all distinctions, titles, [and] every other political measure which lays a burden on the common and poor people for the benefit of the rich."

Morgan supporters (one of whom was the prickly publisher of *The Porcupine's Gazette,* William Cobbett) fired back, warning that "the hour of danger is come. . . . Our government and laws totter under the unremitting exertions of ruffians panting for tumult, plunder and bloodshed . . . and in hellish anticipation [they] view your property as already their own."

Over 8,700 ballots were cast in the reelection, and this time Benjamin Morgan won by 357 votes. The deciding votes came from the Quakers, among Philadelphia's most prosperous and pious citizens, who did not want to see a "grogshop man fixed in the Senate." Israel Israel could be an important part of the power structure during times of distress, the voters seemed to be saying, but he was not welcome there when things returned to normal.

As for Absalom Jones, Richard Allen, and the hundreds of other blacks who nursed the city's sick, they suffered an even worse indignity. On November 13, 1793, just a few days after President Washington's early-morning ride, publisher Mathew Carey issued what would become a best-selling book: *A Short Account of the Malignant Fever, Lately Prevalent in Philadelphia. . . .*

The first edition sold out in nine days, and Carey ran off a second. Seven days later he printed a third. More editions would follow. Carey kept the type in place and ready to go, so it was fairly easy for him to make corrections and to add what he referred to as "improvements." One of the most popular improvements was a necrology, a list of the names of the dead, which began appearing in the third edition.

Readers loved Carey's book. Its style was lively and direct; he presented the fever in all its hideousness and did not spare any details. He began by making readers face the terrible illness: "About this time, this destroying scourge, the malignant fever, crept in among us." Then he let readers relive the mass flight from the city, see the closed shops and empty streets, and meet suffering fever victims and those who bravely stayed to help them.

There were villains as well, though he did not name names. "Who, without horror, can reflect on a husband deserting his wife . . . in the last agony—a wife unfeelingly abandoning her husband on his death bed—parents forsaking their only children—children ungratefully flying from their parents. . . . Masters hurrying off their faithful servants to Bushhill, even on suspicion of fever . . . servants abandoning tender and humane masters."

Such generalizations offended very few readers. They did not recognize themselves or family members in these scenes. And because Carey took a rather gentle approach to the fugitives—he pointedly referred to them as "friends" and openly welcomed them back—he insured that this sizable, book-loving segment of the population would not feel uncomfortable reading his text.

A drawing of Mathew Carey that was done while he was lecturing in Ireland. (THE HISTORICAL SOCIETY OF PENNSYLVANIA)

Yet despite such a careful approach, Carey did go out of his way to vilify one segment of the population: the black volunteers. At one point in his *Account,* he spoke about the Free African Society offering to procure nurses for the sick under the direction of Jones, Allen, and Gray. Then, without describing the daunting task faced by black nurses or praising them for acting fearlessly when everyone else had fled in terror, he attacked them. "The great demand for nurses afforded an opportunity for imposition," Carey stated, "which was eagerly seized by some of the vilest of the blacks. They extorted two, three, four, even five dollars a night for attendance, which would have been well paid by a single dollar. Some of them were even detected in plundering the houses of the sick."

Carey ended this paragraph on a note of restraint, admitting that it would be "wrong to call a censure on the whole for this sort of conduct," because "the services of Jones, Allen, and Gray, and others of their colour, have been great, and demand public gratitude."

Jones and Allen were justifiably shocked and angered by Carey's comments. His condemnation was severe and wide-ranging, while his praise seemed like a grudging afterthought: Hundreds of blacks had come to their white neighbors' aid, so why not say so? And why didn't Carey praise blacks with the same ringing prose he used to praise the committee (of which Carey was a member)?: "I trust that the gratitude of [the committee's] fellow-citizens will remain as long as the memory of their beneficent conduct, which I hope will not die with the present generation."

Jones and Allen answered Carey with a book of their own, published in January 1794: *A Narrative of the Proceedings of the Black People, During the Late Awful Calamity in Philadelphia, in the Year 1793: and a Refutation of Some Censures, Thrown upon Them in Some Late Publications.*

The *Narrative* is not just a firsthand account of what the free black community in Philadelphia did for the sick and dying of the city; it is the very first document published in the United States in which leaders of the black community confronted an accuser directly and attempted to articulate the depth of their anger. It is a remarkable essay, tightly argued and organized, passionate and unrelenting.

It begins by describing how blacks were asked to become involved in the crisis, detailing in dramatic fashion what they did. It then goes on to address and counter every negative statement and implication made by Carey.

The charge of extortion and gouging the sick for more money was particularly painful to the two leaders. Here they pointedly reminded Carey that when these accusations had first surfaced in September, they had been answered to everyone's satisfaction (as he, a member of the committee, should have recalled). In fact, Mayor Clarkson had agreed that the vast majority of black nurses were doing their work both competently and honestly.

"That some extravagant prices were paid, we admit," wrote Jones and Allen, "but how came they to be demanded?" The answer was that white people had driven the prices higher by "over-bidding one another" for the services of the few black nurses available. Again, this was something Jones and Allen had explained to the mayor's satisfaction and that Carey should know about. Why didn't he mention this?

What is more, they argued, "we know as many whites who were guilty" of taking advantage of the sick, "but this is looked over, while the blacks are held up to censure." They then cited examples to illustrate their point. There was an instance where five whites charged $43 to put a corpse in a coffin and haul it downstairs to a waiting wagon. It was a white nurse who stole the valuables of her two dead patients, Mr. and

A

NARRATIVE

OF THE

PROCEEDINGS

OF THE

BLACK PEOPLE,

DURING THE LATE

Awful Calamity in Philadelphia,

IN THE YEAR 1793:

AND

A REFUTATION

OF SOME

CENSURES,

Thrown upon them in some late Publications.

BY A. J. AND R. A.

PHILADELPHIA: PRINTED FOR THE AUTHORS,
BY WILLIAM W. WOODWARD, AT FRANKLIN'S HEAD,
NO. 41, CHESNUT-STREET.

1794.

The title page of Absalom Jones and Richard Allen's groundbreaking rebuttal to Mathew Carey's allegations of misconduct by black nurses.

(THE LIBRARY COMPANY OF PHILADELPHIA)

Mrs. Taylor, while another white nurse was discovered in a drunken stupor wearing rings that belonged to the recently dead Mrs. Malony. And there were the numerous white landlords who raised rents during the plague and even evicted tenants who could not afford the increases. Why hadn't Carey referred to *them* by skin color and called *them* the "vilest"? "Is it a greater crime," Jones and Allen asked, "for a black to pilfer, than for a white to privateer?"

Jones and Allen then turned the tables on Carey. "Had Mr. Carey been solicited to such an undertaking, what would he have demanded?" Carey, of course, had been a volunteer on the committee and taken no pay for his time, but the authors of the *Narrative* would not let him fall back on this fact. They pointed out that Carey had fled the city for a while during the plague, then accused him of returning for the purpose of profiteering in his own way: "We believe he has made more money by the sale of his 'scraps' [that is, his book] than a dozen of the greatest extortioners among the black nurses."

Further, they stated that the money their society had collected for making coffins and burying the dead "has not defrayed the expense of wages which we had to pay to those whom we employed." In fact, by their calculations, the Free African Society was out of pocket at least $500.

At another point in his *Account,* Carey dismissed the grave danger the black nurses had faced by saying that "they did not escape the disorder, however, the number of them that were seized with it, was not great," adding that those blacks who did get yellow fever were cured easily. Jones and Allen replied by saying blacks had suffered the fever to the same degree as whites, and that the nurses, despite the offensive nature of the disease and the danger, had stayed with patients at the expense of their own families.

Carey was offended by the countercharges leveled at him in the

Narrative. He was against slavery, he would point out in *The Address of M. Carey to the Public* (1794), and his magazine, *The American Museum,* often ran antislavery articles and included writings by black authors, something most other journals did not do. As to leaving the city, he had done so with the permission of the mayor, and had been gone only a short time to settle some business accounts.

Finally, he had mentioned Jones and Allen by name in his book and praised their selfless behavior. "I would fain ask the reader," Carey demanded, "is this the language of an enemy? Does this deserve railing or reproach? Is it honorable for Jones and Allen to repay evil for good?"

Individual praise wasn't what Jones and Allen had been concerned about. Blacks had offered their services as a group, and yet Carey had not bothered to praise them for this or honor them to the same degree he honored those on the committee. Instead, by broadly condemning black nurses, Carey put the entire black community "in the hazardous state of being classed with those who are called the 'vilest.'"

They were sorry, Jones and Allen had said, if their words seemed harsh or if anything they said gave offense, "but when an unprovoked attempt is made, to make us blacker than we are, it becomes less necessary to be over cautious on this account."

They had concluded with a powerful statement of principle and self-worth. "We have many unprovoked enemies," they told the reader, "who begrudge us the liberty we enjoy, [who] are glad to hear of any complaint against our colour, be it just or unjust; in consequence of which we are more earnestly endeavoring all in our power, to warn, rebuke, and exhort our African friends, to keep conscience void of offense towards God and man; and, at the same time, would not be backward to interfere, when stigmas or oppression appear pointed at, or attempted against them, unjustly; and, we are confident, we shall stand justified in the sight of the candid and judicious, for such conduct."

Jones and Allen had framed their rebuke of Carey as carefully as possible to allow little room for him to dispute their claims. They realized that one response to their *Narrative* would be a dismissive "It's their word against mine."

To counter such a simple response and put an official seal of approval on their analysis of the situation, they ended their book with the words of someone who was both unassailable and white: Matthew Clarkson. The mayor's note to the authors recognized not only Absalom Jones and Richard Allen but all of the people who volunteered under their direction. "I with cheerfulness give this testimony of my approbation of their proceedings," Clarkson wrote. "Their diligence, attention and decency of deportment, afforded me, at the time, much satisfaction."

Carey's only concession to the arguments of Jones and Allen was to add to his book a brief mention that a number of white nurses had also stolen from patients and acted badly in other ways. Again, it seemed too little and too late. The new information did not appear in the main text, only in a footnote, and only in the very last edition printed. He did not eliminate or even soften in the slightest his attack on the black nurses, despite having the type sitting in his printing shop and ready for "improvements."

So life went on in Philadelphia, in many ways changed forever, in many ways sadly the same as before the yellow fever epidemic began. The sidewalks, shops, taverns, churches, and theaters once again filled with people and buzzed with talk and prayer and gossip. Many had had close calls with death and seen it on a daily basis in the streets of their neighborhoods; everyone—even those who had run from the city—considered himself or herself a survivor.

They were a people left scarred, emotionally and physically. Sudden, mass death had stricken their city, and they were no wiser at all about the nature of the killer. They knew only one thing for certain: When next summer's hot, humid weather returned, yellow fever might very well visit their homes again.

THE RELATION OF MOSQUITOES, FLIES, TICKS, FLEAS, AND OTHER ARTHROPODS TO PATHOLOGY.[a]

By G. Marotel.

It is a matter of common knowledge to-day that while there are many arthropods which live a free life, there are also many others which are parasites, causing in man and also especially in the domestic animals many and varied diseases, the origin and nature of some of which have been known for a long time. It would be banal to recall that phthiriasis is caused by lice, and that certain larvæ of Diptera, such as the œstrids, may occasion the disease called myasis.

This old pathogenic rôle, which has been taught to all the medical and veterinary generations of our time, is quite true. But it is not of this that I wish to speak. It is of a new rôle, brought to light only within the last ten years, the importance of which now grows greater every day, for scarcely a month passes, I might almost say not a week, that some work does not appear which adds some unknown fact or new theory relative to it.

It has to do with one of the questions which in the whole range of parasitic pathology can, with the greatest right, claim to be of practical importance. The danger from the arthropods is a direct consequence of their habits. It only exists in connection with those whose habits are to seek association with men and domestic animals, to bite them and to suck their blood.

Everyone knows that a number of species, such as mosquitoes and gadflies, pass a considerable part of their time in flying from one victim to another, in the same manner that bees wander from flower to flower. Let us suppose, then, that in the course of these wanderings one of them happens to fasten itself on an individual affected by a parasitic or bacterial disease, the agent of which lives in the blood. In sucking the blood it absorbs also the germs which are contained in it, and thus is infected. Should it then attack a healthy person there is danger that it will inoculate him with the disease. This is why

[a] Translated by permission from Annales de la Société d'Agriculture, Sciences et Industrie de Lyon, 1906, pp. 279–302.

CHAPTER ELEVEN

"A Modern-Day Time Bomb"

For all of history and all over the globe she has been a nuisance, a pain, and an angel of death.

—Andrew Spielman and Michael D'Antonio, 2001

September 1, 1858. Emotions were running high at the Marine Quarantine Hospital on Staten Island. Major yellow fever epidemics had struck Manhattan and the surrounding towns in 1702, 1731, 1742, and 1743, and then every year from 1791 through 1821. Now, after a gap of 37 years, the fever was back again, infecting and killing more and more people every day.

New York's medical community knew little more about this invisible killer in 1858 than Philadelphia's had in 1793. The one difference was that early in the nineteenth century Manhattan had established very strict quarantine rules. Anyone suspected of having the disease was shipped off immediately to the Quarantine Hospital. There they could recover—or die—well away from the healthy population.

While no one knew the exact origin of yellow fever, most ordinary citizens as well as many medical professionals insisted it was an

Opposite: *From the 1910 translation of Gabriel Marotel's article on the link between disease and certain insects.* (Author's Collection)

imported disease. Very few people wanted to believe that such a terrible killer could originate in their hometown. This belief that the disease was brought in resurfaced wherever the fever struck. In 1793, for instance, most Philadelphians blamed the refugees from Santo Domingo. In Manhattan the Irish were blamed, and the quarantine effort was aimed primarily at weeding out sick Irish immigrants from arriving ships.

The Quarantine Hospital was the country's leading facility for the treatment of yellow fever and highly praised for its cleanliness and safety. But this didn't matter to its neighbors. People living near the

A mob storms the Marine Quarantine Hospital in 1858.

(*HARPER'S WEEKLY*, SEPTEMBER 11, 1858)

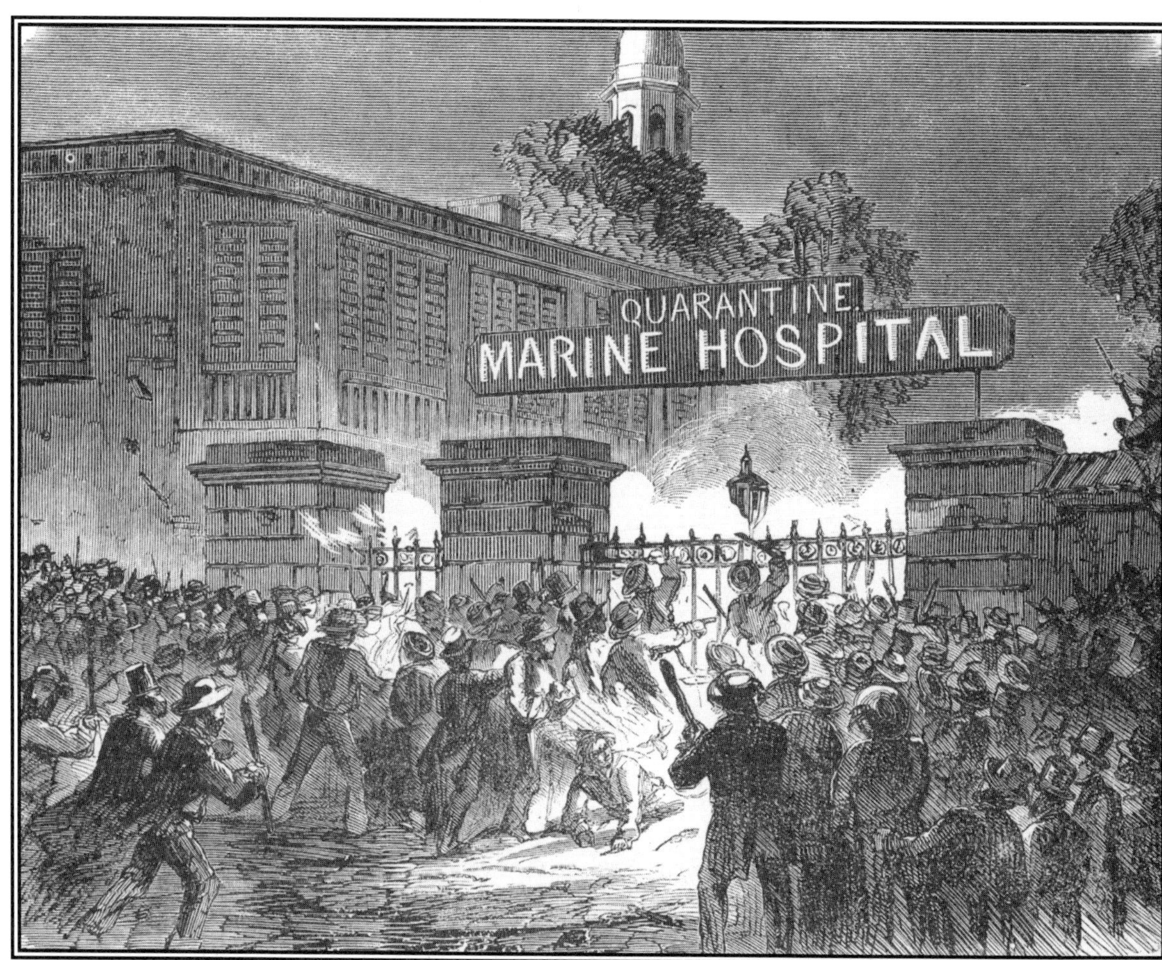

hospital blamed it and its Irish patients for "breeding pestilence" and spreading it throughout the island. As darkness fell on September 1, 1858, angry citizens took matters into their own hands. "About nine o'clock on Wednesday," *Harper's Weekly* reported, "a large party, disguised and armed, assailed the Hospital on two sides at the same time; one squad forced the gate, and the other scaled the wall."

Alarms were sounded, but "before any effective resistance could be offered, the rioters had removed the patients out of the buildings, carrying them bodily up in their mattresses, and depositing them upon the ground some hundred yards from the wards."

Once this was accomplished, the building was set on fire and "burned like a pile of shavings." Next, the resident doctor's house was set afire, followed by a small hospital on a nearby hill. The harbor police and firefighters arrived and managed to put out the latter two fires before the buildings were completely destroyed. The very next day the determined crowd came back and finished burning down the remaining structures.

While *Harper's Weekly* described the efforts of the firefighters and police as "a stirring scene," the magazine's editors were clearly opposed to the presence of the hospital, calling it a "grave injury" to both Staten Island and Manhattan. Some arrests were made, but no one was ever prosecuted for rioting or arson. The specter of yellow fever had incited a normally peaceful group of individuals to violence, and Staten Island officials did not want that mob to turn its fury on them.

Yellow fever terrorized many major cities throughout the 1800s—not only Philadelphia and Manhattan, but Boston, Baltimore, Mobile, Norfolk and Portsmouth, Virginia, Savannah, Charleston, and Jacksonville, to name a few. Nine thousand died in New Orleans in 1853, while Memphis saw 2,000 buried in its 1873 epidemic and another 5,000 in 1878. As late as 1897, letters from the South often arrived with the words "All mail fumigated with formaldehyde" written on them.

Countries outside the United States suffered deadly yellow fever attacks as well. When Toussaint L'Ouverture led a revolt of black Haitian slaves in 1801, Napoleon sent his brother-in-law, General Charles LeClerc, and a military force of approximately 29,000 to crush the rebels. The French killed nearly 150,000 Haitians in their attempt to take back control of the island. Then yellow fever hit the French troops. After 26,000 French soldiers and sailors (including LeClerc) had died, the French packed their tents and left. Haiti was lost to the French, and Napoleon's ambitions for an empire in the New World withered away. Two years later, in 1803, France sold its North American territory to the United States in the Louisiana Purchase.

Epidemics of yellow fever also struck numerous cities in South America, Europe, Russia, and West Africa. Wherever the climate was warm and large groups of people assembled, whether living in established cities or in tents during military campaigns, yellow fever took its toll.

Although millions of fever cases were studied and thousands of autopsies performed, not much new was learned about the disease during the entire nineteenth century. In 1878 the best medical advice a Memphis newspaper could offer frightened readers was: "Keep cool! Avoid patent medicines and bad whiskey! Go about your business as usual; be cheerful and laugh as much as possible."

Doctors were thoroughly baffled by yellow fever, but curiosity and fear drove a number of them to continue to investigate and speculate on its cause, spread, and treatment. In 1848 Dr. Josiah Nott in Alabama noticed that yellow fever receded after swamps were drained off to kill mosquito infestations. Was the mosquito, Nott wondered, the cause of the fever? It's very possible that Nott, in reading about yellow fever epidemics from the past, had come across Rush's mention of those little red spots on patients called petechiae that "resembled moscheto bites."

The idea that such a tiny creature could kill a human was considered preposterous in Nott's day. Besides, Nott did not perform any experiments to prove his theory. It remained an educated guess based on logic and circumstantial evidence and was largely ignored by medical professionals.

One doctor familiar with Nott's theory was intrigued enough to follow up on it. In 1880 Dr. Carlos Finlay of Havana, Cuba, captured mosquitoes and let them ingest the blood of patients suffering from yellow fever. Then, in an experiment that would be considered highly unethical today, he allowed these mosquitoes to feed on healthy humans. To his amazement, 20 percent of the healthy patients soon developed mild cases of the disease.

The following year Finlay presented his conclusions in a paper called "The Mosquito Hypothetically Considered as the Agent of Yellow Fever." His idea certainly received a great deal of attention—almost all of it negative. Because his subjects had not gotten full-blown yellow fever, many scientists thought that Finlay had failed to prove the relationship between mosquitoes and the disease. Some even suggested that he might have seen yellow fever when it wasn't really present in order to support his theory.

It would be more than twenty years before another doctor took Finlay and his work seriously. During those two decades remarkable discoveries were made that changed the entire science of medicine. The 1880s saw two scientists, France's Louis Pasteur and Germany's Robert Koch, isolate various bacteria—extremely small one-celled creatures—living in animals and humans and link them to specific diseases. Then, in the late 1890s, two Germans, Friedrich Löffler and Paul Frosch, discovered other disease-causing organisms even tinier than bacteria, called viruses.

None of these discoveries related specifically to yellow fever. They did, however, put an end to the notion of humors as a medical theory, and they established the possibility that many other diseases might be caused by creatures too small to be seen by the human eye.

It was in 1900 that a young doctor, Jesse Lazear, entered the picture as a member of the U.S. Army Yellow Fever Commission. The commission had been set up in Cuba following the Spanish-American War to discover the cause of yellow fever and develop a cure. Fewer than 400 American soldiers had been killed in the actual fighting on the island, while over 2,000 died of yellow fever. The United States government wanted this deadly enemy identified and eradicated.

Lazear had read Finlay's paper and thought his experiments, while clearly inconclusive, showed promise and should be carried out more fully. In addition, he was aware that in 1898 two scientists working separately had announced that a mosquito was able to carry the malaria parasite and transmit it to humans. A mosquito, Lazear reasoned, might also be the carrier of yellow fever.

None of this impressed Walter Reed, the army doctor who headed the commission. Reed favored the idea that a bacterium, first identified by Italian scientists and usually found in swamps, was the culprit. But to his credit, Reed let Lazear proceed with his experiments on a limited basis.

Lazear's early attempts to show that mosquitoes could transmit the disease from a sick person to a healthy one failed in all but one case. Tests to duplicate this one success also failed until a colleague of his on the commission, James Carroll, caught the disease from an infected insect and nearly died.

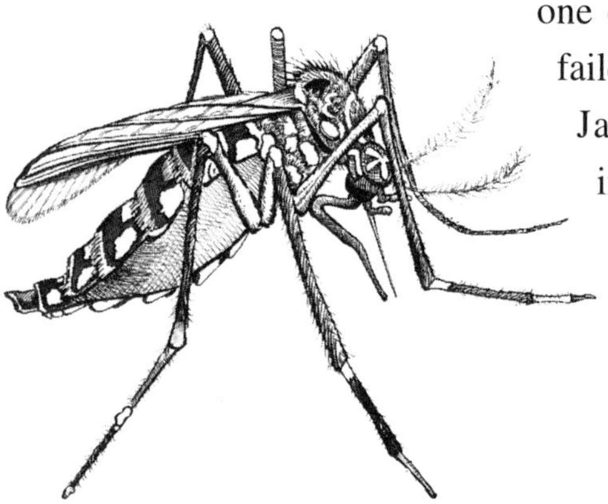

The Aedes aegypti is responsible for infecting approximately 100 million people every year with dengue fever and other diseases.

(Drawing by Rick Parker/Author's Collection)

These two positive results suggested to Lazear that he was very close to proving Finlay's theory. But even with success in sight, Lazear was extremely nervous about potential criticism. Both Nott and Finlay had been dismissed by their medical colleagues, and he did not want to suffer the same sad fate. In a letter to his wife, Lazear cautioned her that "nothing must be said as yet, not even a hint. I have not mentioned it to a soul."

On September 13, 1900, Lazear was in a Havana hospital's yellow fever ward letting mosquitoes feed on patients. As Lazear did his work that day, a mosquito that was not part of his experiment landed on his hand. He thought to shake the insect off, but did not want to interrupt the procedure he was performing. So he watched as the mosquito patiently probed his hand with the cutting part of her proboscis, then sucked his blood for over a minute before flying off.

Two days later Lazear felt ill; two days after this he was confined to bed as yellow fever wracked his body. For eleven days he suffered a high fever, agonizing sweats, and abdominal pain. Black vomit and delirium followed. Finally, on September 25, the thirty-five-year-old doctor died.

James Carroll and another colleague, Aristides Agramonte, felt that Lazear had established a connection between mosquitoes and yellow fever and sent a detailed report of his work to Walter Reed, who was in Washington, D.C., at the time. Reed's initial reaction was anything but encouraging. "I cannot say that any of your cases prove anything," he wrote back to Carroll.

Even so Reed was able once again to push aside his doubts and his own strongly held opinions about how humans contracted the disease. Besides, a dedicated colleague had died for his theory. The least Reed and his team could do was conduct careful tests that would either prove or disprove the idea conclusively.

On his return to Cuba, Reed initiated a series of experiments involving volunteers and insect-tight tents. Healthy subjects spent the night in one tent with a swarm of infected mosquitoes hungry for a meal. In a separate tent other healthy subjects slept wrapped in blankets soiled by the black vomit of patients. Those exposed to the mosquitoes eventually sickened (though, happily, none died); those who slept on the soiled blankets remained healthy. Less than one month after Lazear's death, Walter Reed was able to announce that mosquitoes transmitted the disease and even named the culprit: the female *Aedes aegypti* mosquito (the male of the species prefers plant nectar to blood).

Despite the evidence provided by Reed's commission, many people were still not convinced that the bite of a tiny mosquito could cause a fatal illness. The *Washington Post* denounced the findings in a November 2, 1900, editorial: "Of all the silly and nonsensical rigmarole of yellow fever that has yet found its way into print—and there has been enough of it to build a fleet—the silliest beyond compare is to be found in the arguments and theories generated by a mosquito hypothesis."

Fortunately, scientists in other parts of the world were able to verify the commission's experiments and prove the theory. Of course, establishing the *Aedes aegypti* mosquito as the disease carrier, or vector, did not answer all the questions about yellow fever. The actual source of the yellow fever virus—tree-dwelling monkeys in African and American rain forests—was not identified until 1929. And a safe and effective vaccine was not developed until 1937.

But knowing that a mosquito could spread the disease proved vital in Cuba. Patients with yellow fever were isolated in rooms with screens on the windows so that mosquitoes couldn't feed on their infected blood and then transmit the disease to healthy individuals. Next, the breeding areas for *Aedes aegypti* were systematically destroyed.

This mosquito is almost entirely dependent on humans for its breeding areas—the still water found in water barrels, cisterns, canals, ponds, sewers, gutters, and outhouses. Even a tin can with an inch of water in it can be the birthplace of hundreds of hungry and potentially dangerous mosquitoes.

This cartoon shows a very angry Uncle Sam charging "Amos Quito" with various crimes against humanity. (Author's Collection)

It was this dependence that made *Aedes aegypti* the perfect creature to carry yellow fever into Philadelphia in 1793. Its eggs were unwittingly brought aboard ships in water casks, where they hatched into larvae and grew into adult mosquitoes in seven days. These insects were a nuisance, but not dangerous—until they bit a person who'd come aboard with the virus.

During the next twelve days the yellow fever traveled through this mosquito's body until it reached her salivary glands. After that, every time she fed on someone, she discharged some of the virus into her prey. At the time, a transatlantic sailing voyage might take anywhere from one to two months. This meant that passengers and crew were trapped on board with successive generations of diseased insects. When the ship finally docked, the infected mosquitoes flew off to establish new homes, and create new fever victims, near the open "sinks," wells, water barrels, and privies that were everywhere in the city back then.

In Cuba in 1900, the Yellow Fever Commission sent out soldiers to patrol the city of Havana, going street by street, house by house, searching for open water containers that might be breeding spots for *Aedes aegypti*. Anything that could act as a breeding site was either emptied of water or smashed. Larger bodies of water, such as ponds, were treated with larva-killing oil.

A great many citizens felt such measures were harsh and unfair, especially after being fined when mosquito eggs were found on their property. But the campaign proved successful. Within six months yellow fever was all but gone from Havana. If people in 1793's Philadelphia had only listened when "A. B." had explained how to kill off mosquitoes breeding in water barrels, the fever there might have ended weeks sooner, and hundreds, if not thousands, of lives might have been saved.

The same thorough mosquito-control measures were instituted in the Isthmus of Panama, where work to dig a canal to connect the

Atlantic and Pacific Oceans had bogged down. The French had initiated the canal project in 1881 but almost immediately encountered yellow fever and malaria (which is transmitted by a number of species of *Anopheles* mosquitoes). At one point 7,000 of their 19,000 workers were ill with the diseases; by the time the French company halted construction in 1889, more than 30,000 workers and engineers had died.

The United States took over the project in 1904 and encountered the same disease enemies as the French. The difference was that now the United States knew what to do. An aggressive antibreeding area campaign was launched and once again proved to be highly successful. Yellow fever was almost completely eliminated in Panama. Because *Anopheles* mosquitoes have slightly different breeding areas from *Aedes aegypti,* there were still hundreds of cases of malaria. But overall the campaign worked. Only 2 percent of the workers in the U.S.-led project were hospitalized at any one time, compared with 30 percent for the French.

The Havana and Panama campaigns controlled yellow fever and the *Aedes aegypti* mosquito in those regions, but they did not eliminate the disease completely. It continued to terrorize numerous cities, especially in Central and South America. Finally, in 1947, the Pan American Sanitary Bureau (later renamed the Pan American Health Organization) decided to eradicate the mosquito—and thus the disease—in the entire Western Hemisphere.

Along with destroying breeding areas, adult mosquito populations were also attacked with the widespread use of the pesticide dichlorodiphenyl-trichloroethane, better known as DDT, much of it sprayed from planes. By 1962 twenty-one countries declared themselves free of *Aedes aegypti,* and the world seemed very close to ending yellow fever forever. That was when problems began to develop in the United States.

First, experts in mosquito control complained that Congress had not budgeted enough money for the campaign to succeed. Virtually every southern state was infested with *Aedes aegypti,* these experts pointed out, but funds would run out before the job of eradicating the mosquitoes was half completed.

Second, concern about the health risks and environmental problems associated with the use of DDT increased during the 1960s. These fears were given a public platform with the publication of Rachel Carson's *Silent Spring* in 1962. In this groundbreaking book, the author tackled many emerging ecological concerns, such as the environmental dangers associated with radiation. But it was the use of DDT, and its potential health risks to both animals and humans, that grabbed the public's attention.

The book became a best seller and convinced many citizens and politicians of the dangers posed by indiscriminate spraying of DDT and other chemicals. The use of DDT would be banned in the United States in 1972, but the antimosquito campaign had died long before that.

Actually, Carson had predicted that the campaign would fail even if the spraying continued as mosquito-control experts wanted. "Spraying kills off the weaklings," she explained. "The only survivors are insects that have some inherent quality that allows them to escape harm. These are the parents of the new generation, which, by simple inheritance, possess all the qualities of toughness inherent in its forebears." In other words, supermosquitoes were being created that were capable of resisting DDT.

Careful testing established that it takes about seven years for this new mosquito to emerge and replace the old one. In addition, the same evolutionary process happens when newer pesticides, such as malathion, Sevin, or permethrin, are used.

As this new pesticide-resistant *Aedes aegypti* gradually reestablished itself in Central and South America, another problem was noted. Because the old mosquito—and with it the disease—had been absent so long, hardly anyone had built up an immunity to yellow fever. As a result, hundreds of millions of people were now susceptible to getting yellow fever and other deadly diseases carried by *Aedes aegypti.*

An even more alarming problem was that several mosquito-borne diseases had begun to change. Malaria was the first in which a change was observed. Prior to the 1960s a number of drugs, such as Atabrine and chloroquine, had been developed that effectively treated this illness. Unfortunately, patients would often use only enough of these medicines to reduce the symptoms, saving the rest for future bouts of the disease. Many of the microscopic parasites that produced malaria would survive the sublethal dose and produce offspring capable of withstanding a full dose of the medicine.

This drug-resistant type of malaria began to appear among U.S. troops during the Vietnam War, in which more soldiers were incapacitated by the disease than by battle wounds. Despite the introduction of different, more powerful drugs, the new kind of malaria spread across Asia, then to Africa, and eventually to South America. Today 10 percent of the world's population suffers from malaria every year, resulting in almost three million deaths. In the time it takes to read this sentence, another person has died of malaria.

It's clear now that mosquitoes, animals, and human disease go together. We know that the virus that causes West Nile encephalitis is carried by birds that travel up and down the east coast of the United States and that mosquitoes feed on them and then give the disease to humans. *Aedes albopictus,* better known as the Asian tiger mosquito, sucks the blood of both animals and humans and is capable of carrying a wide variety of viruses, including dengue fever, eastern equine encephalitis, West Nile encephalitis, and LaCrosse encephalitis, all serious illnesses and all potentially lethal to humans. In fact, of the 2,500 kinds of mosquitoes that infest the world, almost 400 of them are capable of transmitting diseases to humans.

"No animal on earth," assert mosquito experts Andrew Spielman and Michael D'Antonio, "has touched so directly and profoundly the lives of so many human beings. . . . With their glassy wings, delicate legs, and seemingly fragile bodies, mosquitoes are nevertheless a powerful, even fatal, presence in our lives."

Which brings us back to *Aedes aegypti* and yellow fever. The disease exists anywhere there are monkey populations, as does the pesticide-resistant mosquito that can transport the disease to humans. As new roads are cut into virgin rain forests, more and more people enter areas where they can become infected. A car ride takes that newly infected person to a major city, where more *Aedes aegypti* mosquitoes wait to feed on him, then carry the disease to another and another and another person. A plane ride carries one of these infected persons to a new country, where still more *Aedes aegypti* wait to feed and fly off.

Two factors make the situation especially dire in the United States. First, no company here has produced the vaccine in recent years. If the disease invaded a large city and a call went out for hundreds of thousands of doses of the vaccine, it would take months to produce it. The U.S. Institute of Medicine studied the situation in 1992 and estimated that an outbreak of yellow fever in a city like New Orleans would infect 100,000 people and kill at least 10,000 of them before it could be brought under control.

Second, despite years of research, *there is still no cure for yellow fever.* While modern medicines can lessen the impact the disease has on the human body, once a person has yellow fever, he or she will have to endure most of the horrible symptoms that Philadelphia's people suffered in 1793.

"Once urban transmission begins in the American region," Duane Gubler, a director at the Centers for Disease Control, warns, "it's probably going to spread very rapidly throughout the region to other urban centers and then from there to Asia and the Pacific." In other words, yellow fever is a "modern-day time bomb. We're just sitting here waiting for it to happen."

The situation is the kind that produces nightmares in thoughtful people. Yet the history of yellow fever offers hope. We know, for instance, that Benjamin Rush was alert enough to recognize the disease before it had spread much beyond Water Street and sounded an alert. Modern doctors should be able to spot yellow fever and issue warnings even sooner.

We know, too, that the antimosquito breeding campaigns in Cuba and Panama were very effective in halting the infections and that massive insecticide campaigns can control the populations of *Aedes aegypti.* Prompt warning and fast (if unpleasant) action have kept yellow fever and related diseases in check over recent decades as well, and the same will be true in the future. Meanwhile, dedicated scientists develop theories and test them, hoping to discover a safe and effective cure.

Yet, if the history of yellow fever tells us anything, it is that this is a struggle with no real end. Yellow fever as we know it now might be conquered, but another version of the disease will eventually emerge to challenge us again. And when it does, we will have to overcome our fears and be prepared to confront it.

SOURCES

While researching *An American Plague,* I consulted a great many books, newspapers, magazines, personal journals, and letters. Below is a select list of sources, arranged by broad subject categories. While most of the titles are self-explanatory, I've provided some personal comments on a few. I hope this will make it easier for curious readers to learn more about various topics covered in these pages.

Firsthand Accounts: Nonmedical

Biddle, Henry D., ed. *Extracts from the Journal of Elizabeth Drinker, from 1759 to 1807, A.D.* Philadelphia: J. B. Lippincott Company, 1889.

Elizabeth Drinker was an avid journal keeper, taking note of what was happening around her in lively and dramatic writing. My favorite entry isn't even from the period of the fever, but from March 1799. That was when the Drinkers were having their privy cleaned, or as Elizabeth put it, "removing the offerings from ye temple of Clacine." The workmen, it seems, ate their meals while in the pit!

Cappon, Lester J., ed. *The Adams-Jefferson Letters.* Chapel Hill, N.C.: University of North Carolina Press, 1959.

Adams's genuine fear of Genêt's activities and the Philadelphia street riots are made very clear in Volume 2, pp. 346–47.

Carey, Mathew. *A Short Account of the Malignant Fever, Lately Prevalent in Philadelphia: With a Statement of the Proceedings That Took Place on the Subject, in Different Parts of the United States, To Which Are Added, Accounts of the Plague in London and Marseilles; and List of the Dead, from August 1, to the Middle of December, 1793,* 1st and 3rd editions. Philadelphia: Mathew Carey, 1793.

Aside from unfairly condemning the black nurses, this short history with a very long title is probably the best overall firsthand account of the fever. Leafing through the necrology, seeing page after page of the names of the dead, gives a true sense of the immensity of this disaster.

———. The Address of M. Carey to the Public. Philadelphia: Mathew Carey, 1794.

Cresson, Joshua. *Meditations Written during the Prevalence of the Yellow Fever in the City of Philadelphia in the Year 1793.* London: W. Phillips, 1803.

Cresson is good at documenting how outlying communities often turned away—sometimes using violence—those fleeing Philadelphia.

Helmuth, J. Henry C. *A Short Account of the Yellow Fever in Philadelphia: For the Reflecting Christian.* Translated from the German by Charles Erdmann. Philadelphia: Jones, Hoff & Derrick, 1794.

His aim was to convince readers that the fever was a warning from God for the sins of the entire community. One way he attempted to do this was by writing detailed "you are there" scenes of the devastation.

Heston, Isaac. "Letter from a Yellow Fever Victim, Philadelphia, 1793," ed. Edwin B. Bonner, *Pennsylvania Magazine of History and Biography,* 86 (1962): 205–7.

Heston's letter touches on numerous aspects of the epidemic—the fact that many newspapers had ceased to publish, that doctors were arguing, and that the streets were empty and desolate. At one point he wrote: "But through all the dainger, thanks be to god, we have yet been preserved, but how long It may continue so, it is impossible to say, for this hour we may be well, and ne[x]t find our selves past recovery." Ten days after writing this, Isaac Heston died of yellow fever.

Jones, Absalom, and Richard Allen. *A Narrative of the Proceedings of the Black People, During the Late Awful Calamity in Philadelphia, in the Year 1793: and a Refutation of Some Censures, Thrown upon Them in Some Late Publications.* Philadelphia: Printed for the Authors, by William W. Woodward, 1794.

There are at least two facsimile versions of this remarkable work available: Philadelphia: Franklin Court Print Shop & Bindery, 1979, and Philadelphia: Independence National Historical Park, 1993.

Miller, Lillian B., ed. *The Selected Papers of Charles Willson Peale and His Family, Vol. 2, Parts 1 and 2.* New Haven, Conn.: Yale University Press, 1988.

Minutes of the Proceedings of the Committee . . . to Attend to and Alleviate the Sufferings of the Afflicted with the Malignant Fever, Prevalent, in the City and Its Vicinity, With an Appendix. Philadelphia: Printed by R. Aitken, 1794.

Iron merchant Caleb Lownes kept the minutes of the committee, recording in his neat handwriting the day-to-day problems he and its other members had to deal with. He missed only two meetings during the epidemic.

Stearns, Samuel. *An Account of the Terrible Effects of the Pestilential Infection in the City of Philadelphia.* Providence, R.I.: William Child, 1793.

Winchester, Elhanan. *Wisdom Taught by Man's Mortality; Or the Shortness and Uncertainty of Life: Adapted to the Awful Visitation of the City of Philadelphia, by the Yellow Fever, in the Year 1793.* Philadelphia: R. Folwell, 1795.

FIRSTHAND ACCOUNTS: MEDICAL

Biddle, Alexander. *Old Family Letters Relating to the Yellow Fever.* Privately printed, 1892.

A collection of all the letters Benjamin Rush wrote to his wife, Julia, from the end of August to mid-November 1793. A copy of this volume, with notes by Lyman H. Butterfield, can be found at the Free Library in Philadelphia.

Butterfield, L. H., ed. *Letters of Benjamin Rush.* Princeton, N.J.: Princeton University Press, 1951.

Rush was headstrong and stubborn, but he reveals many other sides of his personality in these letters to family and friends.

Cathrall, Isaac. *A Medical Sketch of the Synochus Maligna, or Malignant Contagious Fever, as It Lately Appeared in the City of Philadelphia.* Philadelphia: T. Dobson, 1794.

A detailed examination of the disease's symptoms and possible causes, along with Cathrall's treatment, which included throwing cold water over the patient's head every morning and evening; he also warns readers never to tell patients they have yellow fever, because "I have known a patient [to] faint in this disease from an unguarded expression, and afterwards die apparently from a slight attack."

Currie, William. *A Description of the Malignant, Infectious Fever Prevailing at Present in Philadelphia.* Philadelphia: Thomas Dobson, 1793.

Provides a very clear and detailed description of the symptoms of the disease, plus his reasons for believing it was an imported illness.

Devèze, Jean. *An Enquiry into, and Observations upon the Causes and Effects of the Epidemic Disease, which Raged in Philadelphia From the Month of August till Towards the Middle of December, 1793.* Philadelphia: Pierre Parent, 1794.

Contains a description of his gentle medical treatment of fever victims. Devèze was one of the few doctors who worried that rainwater might carry injurious vapors into well water.

Nassy, David. *Observations on the Cause, Nature, and Treatment of the Epidemic Disorder, Prevalent in Philadelphia.* Translated from the French. Philadelphia: Parker and Co., for Mathew Carey, 1793.

Argues that Philadelphia is normally a very healthy city, so the fever must have been imported.

Rush, Benjamin. *Medical Inquiries and Observations,* 2nd edition. Philadelphia: J. Conrad and Co., 1805.

Contains the entire text of his *Account of the Bilious Remitting Yellow Fever, as It Appeared in the City of Philadelphia, in the Year 1793.* Despite the passage of twelve years, Rush has the same firm belief in his cure as he did in 1793.

ALL ABOUT YELLOW FEVER

Bean, William B. *Walter Reed: A Biography.* Charlottesville, Va.: University Press of Virginia, 1982.

Blake, John. "Yellow Fever in Eighteenth-Century America." New York: *Bulletin of the New York Academy of Medicine,* 44 (1968): 673–86.

"The Burning of the Quarantine Hospital on Staten Island." *Harper's Weekly,* September 11, 1858.

Coleman, William. *Yellow Fever in the North: The Methods of Early Epidemiology.* Madison, Wis.: University of Wisconsin Press, 1987.

Opens with a clinical discussion of yellow fever and how the disease travels from the forest to cities, followed by histories of three European outbreaks.

Duffy, John. *The Sword of Pestilence: The New Orleans Yellow Fever Epidemic of 1853.* Baton Rouge, La.: Louisiana State University Press, 1966.

Ellis, John H. *Yellow Fever and Public Health in the New South.* Lexington, Ky.: The University Press of Kentucky, 1992.

How concern and fear in the nineteenth century led to the establishment of health codes, hospitals, and other government measures to protect citizens from this disease.

Estes, J. Worth, and Billy G. Smith, eds. *A Melancholy Scene of Devastation: The Public Response to the 1793 Philadelphia Yellow Fever Epidemic.* Philadelphia: Science History Publications/USA, 1997.

Ten scholars discuss a wide variety of issues relating to the epidemic—from the impact of the newspapers to Rush's cure to the unfair treatment of the black nurses that resulted in Jones and Allen's *Narrative.* Includes a full-color painting of a nineteenth-century patient with yellow fever, black vomit and all.

Horsman, Reginald. *Josiah Nott of Mobile: Southerner, Physician, and Racial Theorist.* Baton Rouge, La.: Louisiana State University Press, 1987.

Humphreys, Margaret. *Yellow Fever and the South.* New Brunswick, N.J.: Rutgers University Press, 1992.

No disease alarmed Southerners in the nineteenth century more than yellow fever, and this book tells why. Also includes many of the erroneous theories developed to explain the cause of the disease, as well as discussions of the work done by Josiah Nott and Carlos Finlay.

Kelly, Howard A. *Walter Reed and Yellow Fever.* New York: McClure, Phillips & Co., 1906.

Kiple, Kenneth F., ed. *The Cambridge World History of Human Disease.* New York: Cambridge University Press, 1993.

Contains a very concise section on yellow fever through the ages.

Marotel, Gabriel. *The Relation of Mosquitoes, Flies, Ticks, Fleas, and Other Arthropods to Pathology.* Washington, D.C.: Government Printing Office, 1910.

Mitchell, John. "Account of the Yellow Fever which Prevailed in Virginia in the Years 1737, 1741, and 1742, in a Letter to the Late Cadwallader Colden, Esq. of New-York." New York: *American Medical & Philosophical Register* 4, 1814.

Benjamin Franklin gave Rush a copy of this 1744 letter, from which Rush conceived his controversial cure.

Patterson, K. David. "Yellow Fever Epidemics and Mortality in the United States, 1693–1905." *Social Science and Medicine,* 34 (1992): 855–65.

Powell, J. H. *Bring Out Your Dead: The Great Plague of Yellow Fever in Philadelphia in 1793.* Philadelphia: The University of Pennsylvania Press, 1949.

A scholarly page-turner—active, dramatic, and suspenseful. Incidentally, Powell makes very clear in his notes that no one went around Philadelphia crying "Bring Out Your Dead," even though some residents and a few irresponsible historians insist that they did.

Winslow, Charles-Edward Amory. *The Conquest of Epidemic Disease: A Chapter in the History of Ideas.* Madison, Wis.: The University of Wisconsin Press, 1980.

Covers a wide range of diseases but takes a very detailed look at the mystery surrounding yellow fever and the many attempts to explain its origins. Also has sections on Pasteur and germ theory and on the discovery that insects can transmit disease to humans.

YELLOW FEVER: FICTION

Anderson, Laurie Halse. *Fever, 1793.* New York: Simon & Schuster, 2000.

A very good book for young readers ten years old and up.

Brown, Charles Brockden. *Arthur Mervyn, or, Memoirs of the Year 1793,* 2 Vols. Port Washington, N.Y.: Kennikat Press, 1963.

This novel was originally published in two sections in 1799 and 1800 and provides an eerie look at a city abandoned by most of its citizens and isolated from the surrounding world by disease.

Fleischman, Paul. *Path of the Pale Horse.* New York: HarperCollins, 1983.

Another good book for young readers.

DOCTORING IN THE OLD DAYS

Cooper, David Y. III, and Marshall A. Ledger. *Innovation and Tradition at the University of Pennsylvania School of Medicine: An Anecdotal Journey.* Philadelphia: University of Pennsylvania Press, 1990.

Includes a section on the medical accomplishments of Benjamin Rush, as well as describing the contributions of other doctors from his era.

Duffy, John. *From Humors to Medical Science: A History of Medical Science.* Chicago: University of Illinois Press, 1993.

Follows the practice of medicine in America from its rather primitive beginnings to the present. Includes discussions of eighteenth-century "do-it-yourself" medicine and very early ideas of germ theory.

Flexner, James Thomas. *Doctors on Horseback: Pioneers of American Medicine.* New York: Fordham University Press, 1992.

Has a chapter on the life and work of Benjamin Rush entitled "Saint or Scourge." This is a balanced view of the man's actions during the 1793 epidemic, taking him to task for his headstrong, bullying ways but reminding readers that his medical decisions were not so outlandish at the time, especially to the desperate and trapped citizens of Philadelphia.

Gates, Phil. *Medicine.* History News series. Cambridge, Mass.: Candlewick Press, 1997.

A lively, illustrated look at medical care throughout the ages. After reading this history, you will be very happy you are living in the twenty-first century.

Meyer, Clarence. *American Folk Medicine.* Glenwood, Ill.: Meyerbooks, Publisher, 1973.

Contains hundreds of cures using herbs, roots, oils, and tree barks for just about anything that ails you. In 1805 Dr. Samuel Thomson recommended that people chew ginger root and swallow the juices to guard the stomach against getting yellow fever.

Murphy, Lamar Riley. *Enter the Physician: The Transformation of Domestic Medicine, 1760–1860.* Tuscaloosa, Ala.: The University of Alabama Press, 1991.

Shows the relationship between the at-home healer and the medical profession, in which even someone like Benjamin Rush sought advice on doctoring from his patients and their relatives.

Nuland, Sherwin B. *The Mysteries Within: A Surgeon Reflects on Medical Myths.* New York: Simon & Schuster, 2000.

Has a very nice discussion of the humoral theory and the effect of humors on different organs of the body.

Starr, Douglas. *Blood: An Epic History of Medicine and Commerce.* New York: Alfred A. Knopf, Inc., 1998.

How people viewed their own blood, from ancient times to the present. Includes mention of Benjamin Rush and his fame as a bleeder.

Williams, Guy. *The Age of Agony: The Art of Healing, 1700–1800.* Chicago: Academy Chicago Publishers, 1975.

A very appropriate title. This survey of doctoring in the United States and

Europe makes it clear why people often turned to neighbors for painless (and free) medical advice.

——. *The Age of Miracles: Medicine and Surgery in the Nineteenth Century.* Chicago: Academy Chicago Publishers, 1981.

Explains how medical techniques slowly changed for the better, including a discussion of the discovery of insects as disease vectors.

PHILADELPHIA, THEN AND AFTER

Benjamin, Lewis Saul. *The Life and Letters of William Cobbett in England & America, Based Upon Hitherto Unpublished Family Papers.* New York: John Lane Co., 1913.

Cobbett was the spiritual father of the "agrarian movement," which is still preached today by some; in addition, his writings, especially those about Benjamin Rush, are often taught in college courses as examples of slashing prose.

Blake, Nelson Manfred. *Water for the Cities: A History of the Urban Water Supply Problem in the United States.* Syracuse, N.Y.: Syracuse University Press, 1956.

Cotter, John L., Daniel G. Roberts, and Michael Parrington. *The Buried Past: The Archaeological History of Philadelphia.* Philadelphia: University of Pennsylvania Press, 1992.

A truly remarkable book. While describing the many digs in and around Philadelphia—including those of privies—the authors reveal a great deal about this city and its people from prehistoric times to the present. Includes details about Washington's residences in Philadelphia and Germantown, the markets, what typical houses looked like, and the creation of the city's water system.

Davies, Benjamin. *Some Account of the City of Philadelphia. . . .* Philadelphia: Richard Folwell, 1794.

A description of the social and economic structure of Philadelphia.

Davis, Allen F., and Mark H. Haller, eds. *The Peoples of Philadelphia: A History of Ethnic Groups and Lower-Class Life, 1790–1940.* Philadelphia: Temple University Press, 1973.

Nice explanation of how Philadelphia's narrow streets and alleys came into existence, plus a look at crime at the end of the eighteenth century and Israel Israel's stolen election. Chapters on many ethnic groups as well.

Driver, Clive E., ed. *Passing Through: Letters and Documents Written in*

Philadelphia by Famous Visitors. Philadelphia: The Rosenbach Museum & Library, 1982.

Hardie, James. *The Philadelphia Directory and Register . . .* , 2nd edition. Philadelphia: Jacob Johnson, 1794.

For 62½ cents you could buy an alphabetical listing of every resident of Philadelphia, which included a job description and address. One entry reads: "Washington George, President of the United States, 190, High St."

Latrobe, Benjamin Henry. *View of the Practicability and Means of Supplying the City of Philadelphia with Wholesome Water.* Philadelphia: Zachariah Poulson, Jr., Printer, 1799.

Looney, Robert F. *Old Philadelphia in Early Photographs, 1839–1914*. New York: Dover Publications, Inc., 1976.

While obviously none of these photographs depict scenes from 1793, they do evoke a sense of a city made up of brick and slate and very narrow alleyways.

Miller, Richard G. *Philadelphia—The Federalist City: A Study of Urban Politics, 1789–1801*. Port Washington, N.Y.: Kennikat Press, 1976.

Thompson, Peter. *Rum Punch & Revolution: Taverngoing & Public Life in Eighteenth-Century Philadelphia*. Philadelphia: University of Pennsylvania Press, 1999.

According to Thompson, news could travel around Philadelphia faster by way of tavern gossip than via the newspapers. Among the favorite spots in town were the London Coffee House (which served more than just coffee), the Pennypot Tavern, and the Man Full of Trouble Tavern.

Warner, Sam Bass, Jr. *The Private City: Philadelphia in Three Periods of Growth*. Philadelphia: University of Pennsylvania Press, 1968.

How the average person spent his or her day, plus a detailed look at the development of the water system.

Weigley, Russell F., ed. *Philadelphia: A 300-Year History.* New York: W. W. Norton, 1982.

Wildes, Harry Emerson. *Lonely Midas: The Story of Stephen Girard*. New York: Farrar & Rinehart, Inc., 1943.

George Washington and His Problems

Abbot, W. W., and Dorothy Twohig, eds. *The Papers of George Washington: The Journal of the Proceedings of the President, 1793–1797*. Charlottesville, Va.: The University Press of Virginia, 1981.

Freeman, Douglas Southall. *George Washington: A Biography.* New York: Charles Scribner's Sons, 1948–57.

This is a series of volumes, seven in all, that covers just about every aspect of George Washington's life, including his problems with Edmond Genêt and his concern over calling Congress into session during Philadelphia's yellow fever epidemic.

Jackson, Donald, and Dorothy Twohig, eds. *The Diaries of George Washington,* Vol. VI, January 1790–December 1799. Charlottesville, Va.: The University Press of Virginia, 1979.

Pickering, Timothy. Letter to George Washington, October 28, 1793. Original in the Library of Congress.

Randolph, Edmund. Letter to George Washington, October 26, 1793. Original in the Library of Congress.

Trumball, Jonathan. Letter to George Washington, October 31, 1793. Original in the Library of Congress.

Washington, George. Letters of 1793: to Alexander Hamilton, September 25 and October 14; to Thomas Sim Lee, October 13; to Jonathan Trumball, October 13; to Oliver Wolcott, October 14; to James Madison, October 14; to Timothy Pickering, October 14; to Edmund Randolph, October 14 and October 23; to Henry Knox, October 15. Originals in the Library of Congress.

BLACKS IN PHILADELPHIA

Allen, Richard. *Life, Experience and Gospel Labours.* Philadelphia: Martin and Boden, Printers, 1833.

Allen recounts the incident where white members of St. George's tried to make him and other blacks sit in the back of the church and how this prompted him to organize his own church.

Douglass, William. *Annals of the First African Church, in the United States of America, Now Styled the African Episcopal Church of St. Thomas, Philadelphia. . . .* Philadelphia: King & Baird, 1862.

Du Bois, W. E. B. *The Philadelphia Negro: A Social Study.* New York: Benjamin Blom, 1965.

Hornsby, Alton, Jr. *Chronology of African-American History: Significant Events and People from 1619 to the Present.* Detroit: Gale Research, Inc., 1991.

Does not mention the yellow fever epidemic but has information about the lives of Richard Allen and Absalom Jones, as well as specific references to blacks in Philadelphia.

Kaplan, Sidney. *The Black Presence in the Era of the American Revolution, 1770–1800.* Greenwich, Conn.: New York Graphic Society Ltd. and Smithsonian Institution Press, 1973.

Nash, Gary B. *Forging Freedom: The Formation of Philadelphia's Black Community, 1720–1840.* Cambridge, Mass.: Harvard University Press, 1988.

That Buzzing in Your Ear

Carson, Rachel. *Silent Spring.* Boston: Houghton Mifflin, 1962.

This book alerted a large audience to a variety of environmental problems, spurring changes in our laws affecting the air, land, and water. Still important reading after forty years.

Spielman, Andrew, and Michael D'Antonio. *Mosquito: A Natural History of Our Most Persistent and Deadly Foe.* New York: Hyperion Books, 2001.

You might not think it from the title, but this is an extremely entertaining and informative book—not to mention scary.

Taubes, Gary. "A Mosquito Bites Back." *The New York Times Magazine,* August 24, 1997.

Essentially, this article tells you that mosquitoes are out there and dangerous and it won't be long before they're living in your backyard.

Other Plagues

Here is a list of books dealing with a variety of killer diseases. Some of them are transmitted by mosquitoes, some by other insects, such as ticks and fleas, and still others through person-to-person contact. The one thing they all have in common is that they are deadly.

Bourdain, Anthony. *Typhoid Mary: An Urban Historical.* New York: Bloomsbury Publishing, 2001.

How a cook named Mary Mallon gave this deadly disease to the people she worked for and then led health officials and police on a lively chase.

Defoe, Daniel. *A Journal of the Plague Year.* Harmondsworth, Great Britain: Penguin Books, Ltd., 1966.

I love reading about the bubonic plague, sometimes called the Black

Death. While this book is fictional in nature, it is filled with a great deal of information about day-to-day life with death all around you.

Duffy, John. *Epidemics in Colonial America.* Baton Rouge, La.: Louisiana State University Press, 1953.

What our ancestors suffered.

Fenn, Elizabeth A. *Pox Americana: The Great Smallpox Epidemic of 1773–82.* New York: Hill and Wang, 2001.

What Native Americans and the Continental soldiers under George Washington suffered.

Garrett, Laurie. *The Coming Plague: Newly Emerging Diseases in a World Out of Balance.* New York: Penguin Books, 1994.

What we and our children will suffer.

Giblin, James Cross. *When Plague Strikes: The Black Death, Smallpox, AIDS.* New York: HarperCollins Publishers, 1995.

A wonderfully written look at three epidemics and how people and doctors reacted in times of fear and uncertainty.

Hays, J. N. *The Burdens of Disease: Epidemics and Human Response in Western History.* New Brunswick, N.J.: Rutgers University Press, 1998.

A sweeping history of many of the world's most deadly diseases and their effects on society.

Kohn, George C., ed. *Encyclopedia of Plague and Pestilence.* New York: Facts on File, Inc., 1995.

An A-to-Z history of many different plagues from many different places around the world.

Kraut, Alan M. *Silent Travelers: Germs, Genes, and the "Immigrant Menace."* Baltimore, Md.: The Johns Hopkins University Press, 1995.

Many ailments are covered here, with emphasis on how the accompanying fear and panic have often resulted in oppression of helpless groups of people.

McNeill, William H. *Plagues and Peoples.* New York: History Book Club, 1993.

How a variety of epidemics have shaped human history.

Oldstone, Michael B. A. *Viruses, Plagues, & History.* New York: Oxford University Press, 1998.

A history of a number of the "old" diseases, including yellow fever, as well as many of the newer scourges, such as Ebola, HIV/AIDS, and mad cow disease (bovine spongiform encephalopathy).

Porter, Stephen. *The Great Plague.* Trowbridge, Great Britain: Redwood Books, 2000.

Presents the bubonic plague as it kills off over 70,000 Londoners in 1665, and thousands more in the suburbs. Contains some marvelously grim illustrations.

Rosenberg, Charles E. *The Cholera Years: The United States in 1832, 1849, and 1866.* Chicago: University of Chicago Press, 1962.

Rosner, David, ed. *Hives of Sickness: Public Health and Epidemics in New York City.* New Brunswick, N.J.: Rutgers University Press, 1995.

As New York City grew larger and larger in the nineteenth and twentieth centuries, many epidemics, including yellow fever, followed.

Shilts, Randy. *And the Band Played On: Politics, People, and the AIDS Epidemic.* New York: St. Martin's Press, 1987.

A chilling history of this modern-day disease.

Sontag, Susan. *Illness as Metaphor.* New York: Farrar, Straus and Giroux, 1978.

Compares and contrasts the nineteenth-century view of tuberculosis with ours of cancer.

Wills, Christopher. *Yellow Fever/Black Goddess: The Coevolution of People and Plagues.* New York: Addison-Wesley Publishing Company, Inc., 1996.

Despite the title, there is hardly a mention of yellow fever in this book. But it contains other killer diseases, such as the Black Death, cholera, typhus, and HIV/AIDS. The caption to a Thomas Nast illustration notes that this famous political cartoonist died of yellow fever while visiting Ecuador in 1902.

Zinsser, Hans. *Rats, Lice and History: Being a Study in Biography, which, after Twelve Preliminary Chapters Indispensable for the Preparation of the Lay Reader, Deals With the Life History of Typhus Fever.* New York: Black Dog & Leventhal Publishers, 1963.

A lighthearted but fact-filled "biography" of typhus fever, with mention of many other fevers and topics, including how yellow fever has been seen to mutate and become even more deadly.

ACKNOWLEDGMENTS

The idea for this book began to take shape more than six years ago, when I came across a copy of John H. Powell's *Bring Out Your Dead.* Reading this book was a revelation, not just because of the depth of scholarship, but because Powell brought the time alive in a powerful and emotional way. I've discovered since that no one writes about the Philadelphia epidemic—no one writes about yellow fever, period!—without relying heavily on this work, and that includes me.

Many people helped me gather information for my text and hunt out appropriate illustrations, and I'd like to thank them for their invaluable assistance: Karie Diethorn, Chief, Museum Branch, Independence National Historical Park; Carol Wotowicz Smith, Historian, The National Grange Mutual Insurance Company/The Green Tree Collection; Stacy Bomento, Rights and Reproductions Department, Philadelphia Museum of Art; Leslie A. Morris, Curator of Manuscripts, and Tom Ford, Public Services, The Houghton Library, Harvard University; Barbara Katus, Registrar, the Pennsylvania Academy of Fine Arts; Laura E. Beardsley, Head of Graphics, The Historical Society of Pennsylvania; Cathy Grophes, The Abby Aldrich Rockefeller Folk Art Museum.

I would also like to thank Charles B. Greifenstein, Curator of Archives & Manuscripts, the College of Physicians of Philadelphia, for his very good advice concerning medical illustrations. The College also houses the Mutter Museum for Infectious Diseases, where I found a rare first edition of Defoe's

Journal of the Plague Year and the illustration of mass burial. The front section of the museum contains an interesting exhibit on a variety of infectious diseases, including yellow fever. The Mutter Museum also houses a collection of medical oddities from the nineteenth century—such as a piece of John Wilkes Booth's neck, 139 skulls, and a medicine cabinet filled with sharp objects people swallowed, or at least tried to swallow. And these aren't the strangest things you'll see if you visit this museum.

Thanks, too, to Jim Giblin, who suggested I check out Charles Willson Peale and his doings during the fever, and whose own wonderful book about epidemics, *When Plague Strikes,* both inspired and challenged me to work harder on my project.

Finally, I would also like to thank Nicole H. Scalessa, Connie King, and Valerie Miller of the Library Company of Philadelphia for their skill and patience in helping me locate books, letters, and newspapers from the period. I especially want to acknowledge the patient guidance provided by Philip Lapsansky, Chief of Reference at the Library Company and curator of its Afro-Americana Collection. I still remember the chill that ran through me when he handed me a copy of Absalom Jones and Richard Allen's *A Narrative of the Proceedings of the Black People, During the Late Awful Calamity in Philadelphia* and said, "This is the actual copy of the *Narrative* Jones and Allen donated to the Library Company in 1794." Reading about our nation's history is one thing; actually holding it in your hands is something altogether different.

A NOTE ABOUT THE ILLUSTRATIONS

Philadelphia in 1793 had a number of talented artists and engravers, including Charles Willson Peale and William Birch, plus a great many printers, and a public eager to know what happened to their city during the yellow fever epidemic. Many books and pamphlets were published about the epidemic, but it seems that no one ever documented it visually. "In fact," Charles Greifenstein, Curator of Archives & Manuscripts at the College of Physicians, told me, "there are very few medical images of any kind from around 1750 until the mid-nineteenth century. Not even of something as common as bleeding."

It's possible that the 1793 plague was so traumatic and the pain so fresh that artists steered clear of it out of respect for the dead and their loved ones. Or maybe they felt the city's image had already taken enough of a beating via the written word. It's also possible that medical practices were so familiar to the general public that images of them were considered redundant. Still, it would have been interesting to peek through the curtain of time and actually see what the streets of Philadelphia were like as Benjamin Rush hurried to a patient's bedside or the Reverend Mr. Helmuth visited yet another sick member of his congregation.

I've tried to include images that will help readers imagine what the city was like back then—the narrow streets, the press of people, and so on. I've also included pictures from Europe to show bloodletting, a typical epidemic scene, and mass burial.

The one illustration I wish I could have included was done by Dr. Carlos

Finlay, the Cuban physician who published his theory that mosquitoes might be the cause of yellow fever twenty years before Walter Reed's commission proved it. Finlay always felt he was not given proper credit for his work and spent many years fighting to establish his contribution. His painting (which can be found on page 57 of Michael Oldstone's *Viruses, Plagues, & History*) shows Walter Reed, James Carroll, and Jesse Lazear in a small but very pleasant office with lush, tropical vegetation just outside the door. Finlay has also painted himself into this picture, a somewhat sad way to include himself in the history of yellow fever.

INDEX

Note: Page numbers in **bold** type refer to illustrations.